A SYMPHONY OF THE CHRISTIAN YEAR

RANDOLPH CRUMP MILLER

1954

GREENWICH · CONNECTICUT

Designed by Stefan Salter

Printed in the United States of America

DEDICATED TO OUR CHILDREN

Barbara Hallett Miller

Frank Vaughan Fowlkes

Phyllis Muriel Miller

Carol Christine Miller

Elizabeth Rives Fowlkes

Muriel Randolph Miller

PREFACE

The Christian year provides a variety of emphases for preaching, so that a rounded view of the Gospel may be presented. Let us look at the Christian year as a symphony, which has a central theme dramatized by the life, death, and resurrection of Jesus Christ, and with variations on that theme from season to season. This musical interpretation is found in the opening sermon. The succeeding sermons approach the themes of the day from textual, topical, and problematical angles. The first half of the book covers sixteen such days.

Our common life contains a nontraditional Christian year, arising from such events as the men's Advent Corporate Communion, Theological Education Sunday, Youth Sunday, and from such cooperative ventures as Race Relations Sunday, Labor Sunday, World-wide Communion Sunday, and Reformation Day.

It is my hope that these selections will appeal to those lay people who find written sermons helpful. Sermons lose something of their essential flavor when they are not heard, and reading them aloud may prove more inspiring than studying them quietly. Originally they were preached at St. Alban's Church, Albany, California.

Lay readers who read sermons while conducting services should find every selection useful on the day indicated, and some will have relevance on almost any Sunday. The sermons for Youth Sunday and Thanksgiving Day can be adapted for a family service where children are present. The suggested psalms, lessons, and hymns are for the guidance of lay readers. The second hymn in each list is especially suitable for use before the sermon.

A concern for Christian education on a parish level runs throughout these sermons. It is my conviction that the approach to Christian education of our Department of Christian Education is sound. There can be education for redemption on a parish-wide level, where our beliefs are made relevant to life and our fellowship is such that we are made upright by faith through grace. This education begins in the home, where parents have the chief responsibility, and it continues throughout one's entire life. These sermons do not stress a one-two-three outline of ethical behavior; instead, they strive to create the atmosphere in which we will become sensitive to the persuasive grace of God in our midst. In so far as we come to have the mind of Christ, God will call us to that action which is worthy of the vocation to which we are called.

A wide use of many translations of the Bible adds to the richness of interpretation of many passages. I am indebted to the publishers who have given permission to quote from their copyrighted works.

In the text, each passage is marked as to its translation as follows:

KJ *King James Version*

RSV *Revised Standard Version* (Copyright 1946 and 1952 by the Division of Christian Education of the National Council of the Churches of Christ in the United States of America)

ASV *American Standard Version* (Copyright 1929 by the International Council of Religious Education)

G *The Bible: An American Translation,* by E. J. Goodspeed and J. M. P. Smith. (Copyright 1939 by the University of Chicago Press)

M *The Moffatt Bible: a New Translation,* by James Moffatt. (Copyright 1922, 1935, and 1950 by Harper and Brothers)

P *The Four Gospels Translated into Modern English* and *Letters to Young Churches,* by J. B. Phillips. (Copyright 1952 and 1947 by The Macmillan Co.)

B *The New Testament in Basic English,* by I. A. Richards, Cambridge University Press

K *The New Testament* in the translation of R. A. Knox. (Copyright 1944 by Sheed and Ward, Inc., New York)

W *New Testament in Modern Speech,* by R. F. Weymouth, Harper

VK *Berkeley Version of the New Testament,* by Gerrit Verkuyl, Zondervan

20 *Twentieth Century New Testament,* Revell (out of print)

PB *Prayer Book,* Seabury

Hymn numbers in the text refer to *The Hymnal, 1940,* and I am grateful to the following authors and owners of copyrights for their kind permission to quote all or parts of their copyrighted hymns:

From *Enlarged Songs of Praise* by permission of the Oxford University Press: Hymns 207, 258, 262, 299, 313, and 521.

From the *Yattendon Hymnal,* edited by Robert Bridges, by permission of the Clarendon Press, Oxford: Hymn 75.

From *The Unutterable Beauty,* by G. A. Studdert-Kennedy, by permission of Hodder and Stoughton, Ltd.: Hymn 156.

From *The Way of Light,* by Howard Chandler Robbins, by permission of Morehouse-Gorham Co.: Hymn 354.

Mrs. Howard Chandler Robbins: Hymn 14.

Mrs. Alexander G. Cummins: Hymn 432.

The Rev. William P. Merrill: Hymns 145, 535.

Erica Oxenham: Hymns 263, 510, 527.

The Rev. F. Bland Tucker: Hymns 68, 366, 504.

RANDOLPH CRUMP MILLER

TABLE OF CONTENTS

Part One

I.

A SYMPHONY OF THE CHRISTIAN YEAR

THE FIRST SUNDAY IN ADVENT

PSALM 50; MALACHI 3:1-6 & 4:4-6; LUKE 1:5-25; HYMNS 2, 235, 258, 4

> This month shall be for you the beginning of months. (Exod. 12:2, RSV)
>
> Let the word of Christ dwell in you richly, as you teach and admonish one another in all wisdom, and as you sing psalms and hymns and spiritual songs . . . in your hearts to God. (Col. 3:16, RSV)

The first Sunday in Advent marks the beginning of the Christian year. It may be helpful and illuminating if we think of the Christian year as a symphony in its expression of a great variety of meanings. There are slow movements and fast movements, loud strains and quiet melodies, transitions and new themes. As we live through this symphony of the Christian year, we respond with appreciation to the various shades of meaning found in the Gospel of Jesus Christ. No popular song, no jazz arrangement, no operatic aria, no chamber music, and no concerto carries within it the variety and richness of a symphony.

Our rhythm of worship is geared to a symphonic arrangement. We never lose sight of the underlying central theme on which are played many variations bringing out the profound depth, the frustrating agonies, the beatific joys, and the ultimate salvation of human souls.

The opening movement is one of expectation, looking forward to the advent of Jesus Christ. The overtones of purple indicate the humility and penitence of men in the face of the great gift that God is about to offer. The brief second movement tells the beautiful Christmas story, and the third movement, following so quickly, tells of the spreading of that message throughout the world in Epiphany. The long fourth movement begins with a transition, full of the dynamic expression of pre-Lent reflected in "he who would valiant be." This leads into the long and introspective tones of self-searching and religious exercise that turn to the depths of tragedy and wickedness before building to the climax of the Resurrection. This movement continues with the Resurrection theme and then stops suddenly with the Ascension. This sharp break is followed by the great confusion of tongues, as the fifth and final movement begins with great fanfare and then subsides into a long period of interpretation of the story. Mingled with this major development of the symphony are many minor explosions in the background, as one life after another is given brief expression in a saint's day.

Think what a composer could do with this if he simply used the hymns of the Church to express the full meanings of Christian living:

"O come, O come, Emmanuel"
"O little town of Bethlehem"
"Christ is the world's true Light"
"He who would valiant be"
"Forty days and forty nights"
"Alone thou goest forth, O Lord, In sacrifice to die"
"The strife is o'er"
"Jesus Christ is risen today"
"See the Conqueror mounts in triumph"
"The Church's one foundation"

"Come, thou Holy Spirit, come"
"Holy, Holy, Holy"

Without the Christian year as a guide, we may get lost in our own popular songs, overplay one theme at the expense of another, reduce the full meaning of the Christian faith to a jazz cult, and therefore fail to see the redemption which draws nigh in Christ Jesus.

Let us, then, take notes on a symphony of the Christian year, touching at least the high spots of Christian worship and service as the major theme is varied by God's commands and men's needs. The major theme is Jesus Christ: "For God so loved the world that he gave his only Son, that whoever believes in him should not perish but have eternal life." (John 3:16, RSV)

I.

Our symphony begins with Advent. It is a perfect opening, looking forward to the great event of the near future. There is an emphasis on the Bible story of looking for the Messiah; there is a recounting of John the Baptist as the forerunner; there is the prophecy of a second coming—all summed up in the words of the second Isaiah:

"The voice of one crying in the wilderness:
Prepare the way of the Lord,
make his paths straight." (Luke 3:4, RSV; cf. Isa. 40:3)

This brief movement is one of penitence, expectation, and hope. The somberness of God's judgment is mixed with the hope of the world's redemption. But the hue is violet. The present age cannot redeem itself, and the future is not yet here. Man is helpless and the world's resources without God are inadequate. Man needs to be baptized "with the Holy Spirit and with fire."

II.

The second movement is full of all the power of the coming of God into human life. Christ the Lord is born! Man has received the "tidings of comfort and joy." Angels, shepherds, and men from the East have acknowledged the birth of one

> ". . . who came in weakness,
> And in a manger lay
> To teach his people meekness?" (Hymn 14)

For the first time, the major theme of the symphony has been announced. It is "good news of a great joy which will come to all the people." God has come into human life in a unique way, and this is the beginning of men's hope.

This movement is even shorter than the first one, for it announces the theme of the world's redemption without the variations. These are postponed for the future development of *A Symphony of the Christian Year.*

III.

> "In Epiphany we trace
> All the glory of his grace." (Hymn 235)

This movement begins with the men who followed the star, providing a recapitulation of the Christmas theme. They followed the light wherever it led them, and far across the plains they came to lay their gifts at the feet of the Christ child. And then there is a subtle and definite change in the music as a new theme breaks in:

> "Christ is the world's true Light . . .
> New life, new hope awakes,

Where'er men own his sway:
Freedom her bondage breaks,
And night is turned to day." (Hymn 258)

From the star over the manger, the music takes us to the light within the stable, and this is "the light that lighteth every man." Here, then, is the drama of the battle of light against darkness. Here is the God of light, called in another religion by the name of Mazda, and lined up against him are all the powers of darkness.

Darkness is to be turned into light throughout the world. Thus, the message of the Epiphany is to take the saving Gospel of Christ to all the nations. The star of Bethlehem becomes the light of the world who is

"The Day-star clear and bright
Of every man and nation." (Hymn 258)

IV.

The transition from Epiphany to Lent strikes three vigorous notes. Here, in quick succession, are the fundamental attitudes of Christian action. Man's reaction to what God has done for him in Christ is seen when man's faith is expressed in obedience.

The vigor of Christian living is reflected in Paul's words: "Do you not know that in a race the runners all compete, but only one wins the prize? That is the way you must run, so as to win. Any man who enters an athletic contest goes into strict training, to win a wreath that will soon wither, but the one we compete for will never wither." (I Cor. 9:24-25, G)

"Am I a soldier of the cross?"
"Awake, my soul, stretch every nerve."
"Come, labor on."

Such a life demands courage, for men are "oft in danger, oft in woe." And it is also a life of love: "So faith, hope, love abide, these three; but the greatest of these is love." (I Cor. 13:13, RSV)

This transition to the fourth movement is varied in its pungent and dynamic meanings. Who can face up to these challenges without feeling gross inadequacy, a need for prayer and penitence, a desire for the grace of God? The ideal is set up for us, but we need to catch our breath and make preparations. Then we can undertake these things by God's grace.

This movement then states its first melodic line of Lenten preparation. The theme is set against the background of the forty days which Jesus spent in the desert when He was tempted to misuse the gifts that His heavenly Father had given Him. Our response is recorded as we turn to our own condition. We, too, must face up to the temptations which are before us. We, too, must make our own preparation so that God will act on us to redeem us from sin.

It is not easy. This music is too tragic to be beautiful, for we see in ourselves the elements in the lives of Jesus' contemporaries that led to His death at their hands. Already, by the fourth Sunday in Lent, we are looking forward to the inevitability of the Crucifixion, because the men who opposed Jesus were like us. We, too, are willing to place straw in His path, but we, too, will not be around when the tragic end comes. Perhaps there must be a cock crowing in the background as we deny Him, or we may have to sing: "Ah, holy Jesus, . . . I crucified thee" (Hymn 71); for the tragic climax comes as we see Him deserted by everyone.

"Alone thou goest forth, O Lord,
In sacrifice to die;
Is this thy sorrow naught to us
Who pass unheeding by?" (Hymn 68)

Now comes the climactic theme of victory, reflecting the turning point of all history and spelling out the assurance of man's redemption. It is no finale, but it is the focal point of all the meaning of God for man. God has acted to reconcile the world to Himself in the life and death and Resurrection of Jesus Christ.

"The strife is o'er, the battle done,
The victory of life is won;
The song of triumph has begun.
Alleluia!" (Hymn 91)

But this climax cannot be the end of this movement. The impact is so great and overpowering that it must taper off slowly. There is a long post-Easter repetition of the Resurrection theme. The living Christ who was alive to the disciples is also alive in us. Heavenly strains dominate the music as we see a cloud cover the intimacy of Jesus' presence. Then, the music comes to a sudden stop.

"See the Conqueror mounts in triumph." (Hymn 103)

V.

There is complete silence before the fifth and final movement begins. The symphony has been dramatic so far because it has dealt primarily with the life of Jesus Christ as reflected in the experience of the disciples. Now there is a difference. The major theme of the life of Christ drops into the background, and the ongoing life of the believers is depicted in a new way.

It begins with sheer confusion. Gone are all the clean-cut lines of melody and harmony, gone are the majestic themes; it sounds more like what occurred at the tower of Babel. There is confusion of tongues as every man hears the disciples speaking in his own language. It is Pentecost. Out of what seems to the doubters to be a drunken brawl comes a brief summary or recapitulation of the entire symphony. Then a new theme is announced in a response as some three thousand are baptized.

> "The Church's one foundation is Jesus Christ her Lord."
> (Hymn 396)

The Holy Spirit is now seen by men to be present among them.

Another summary follows in a reinterpretation of the major theme. This more formal presentation crystallizes the picture of God as Father, Son, and Holy Spirit, with the reminder that God made us, saves us, and makes us holy. He is the Holy Trinity.

This last movement continues at great length. Musically, this last part of the symphony lacks any dramatic climax, for the Trinity season is a teaching season. Much of this finale is like a recitative in an oratorio rather than like the variation of a symphonic theme. Yet, in this longest portion of the symphony there is the constant relating of all the elements of the Gospel story to the redemptive element of everyday living. The richness of various minor episodes, the abundance of faith found in routine living, the concern for being Christian in the little things of life, the solving of personal and social problems, the virtues of humility and faithfulness and mercy, the facing of our own sufferings, the need for compassion and courtesy, getting away from anger, being neighborly, freedom from anxiety, and back finally to the prayer with which the symphony completes the circle:

> "Stir up, we beseech thee, O Lord, the wills of
> thy faithful people." (P.B., p. 225)

A great symphony on these themes could be written for an orchestra, but for those of us who follow the Christian year in our worship this symphony is written on our hearts. All our needs appear from time to time, and the full Gospel of Jesus Christ is presented to us with all its power to save us from sin and damnation. And just as we begin with expectation, so we end by being so stirred up that we will go out from the symphony of our worship to do the will of our heavenly Father who gives us grace through faith in Jesus Christ.

2.

EDUCATION FOR REDEMPTION

SECOND SUNDAY IN ADVENT

PSALM 119:1-16; ISAIAH 55:1-13; II TIMOTHY 3:1-4:2;

HYMNS 401, 403, 133, 402

> All scripture is inspired by God and profitable for teaching, for reproof, for correction, and for training in righteousness, that the man of God may be complete, equipped for every good work. (II Tim. 3:16-17, RSV)
>
> I am reminded of your sincere faith, a faith that dwelt first in your grandmother Lois and your mother Eunice and now, I am sure, dwells in you. (II Tim. 1:5, RSV)

Our Christian faith, which we have inherited from our forefathers, rests on the Bible. Our Christian education is centered in the Biblical faith. Our Christian worship is Biblical in the phrases of its prayers and hymns as well as in its responses and lessons.

It is possible, however, to have Bible study which is not Christian, Church history which is irreligious, Christian behavior which is a form of etiquette, and Christian morality which is not redemptive.

Our understanding of the place of the Bible in our lives turns on the word *redemption.* A boy in church school wrote on his examination paper that "redemption and conversion are banking terms." And so they are. Redemption is derived from the practice of buying back something which formerly belonged to a person. If I pawn my wife's ring, I can redeem it by paying back the money. If my friend goes to jail, I can put up his bond and get him out.

Men are not always able to buy themselves out of their sinful situations, and thus God takes the initiative to free them from their sins. Men are separated from God when they disobey Him. The conditions of worry, nervous strain, and sinful actions get people down. They face moral, mental, and spiritual frustration. And they find that all efforts to overcome these conditions lead to greater frustration. They need redemption, and they lack the price.

I.

Christian education is, first of all, a presentation of the *drama of Redemption.* This is more than Bible study, or character education, or exposure to worship. As we read the Bible, we find it to be a story about God. God and not man is the chief actor. It can be presented in five acts: Creation, Covenant, Christ, Church, and Consummation.

Act I is the spectacular act of Creation, dressed in the imagination of the primitive Hebrews. It tells how God created the earth and all that therein is. He gave us life and mind and the power to make moral choices. Because He gave men freedom, this first act ends with man experimenting with the various ways of disobeying God. The result of the experiment is always the same: men are separated from God when they use their freedom to disobey Him. At the end of this first act, you can see into the minds of men, and as you look you discern turmoil, anxiety, loneliness, frustration, and insecurity. This is not just a myth written by a Hebrew some three thousand years ago; it is your story and my story, and the story of our children.

Act II is the story of the Covenant. Because man in his freedom finds himself separated from God, his loneliness is symbolized when Adam and Eve were cast out of the Garden of Eden. Then,

God entered into an agreement with his people by giving them a law by which they could guide themselves. This law is conveniently summarized in the Ten Commandments. God provided a variety of interpretations, however, and if men found the law too difficult to understand, there were such prophets as Amos and Isaiah to show what the moral law meant in relation to society. God demands righteousness. God is made holy in righteousness.

In this second act, we see men struggling to meet the demands of the law, and they fall short of the requirements. They suffer exile. They are persecuted. They fail to find satisfaction in ceremonial. They find that there is a difference between knowing what is right and doing what is right. The agreement, the covenant, the testament, breaks down.

As the curtain falls on the second act, we can hear the lament of the preacher: "All is vanity. . . . We need a saviour." The prophets cry: "We need a saviour to redeem us from our sins, and from loneliness, and from separation from the holy God." The old agreement needs to be superseded by a new agreement. The old testament needs to be fulfilled by a new testament.

Act III is centered in Christ. God sent His Son. In Jesus Christ, we see a man who lived our life, suffered our temptations, was rejected and lonely and misunderstood, and finally faced death. In this life, we see how much God loves us. In this obedience, we see what human life can be. And yet it ended in sudden, tragic death.

But after death came the experience of the Resurrection. The disciples found that through their faith in the Risen Christ, they had power to overcome their temptations. They were drawn into a new and richer fellowship. They were reconciled with God. So we learn that death is not the end, and that life has eternal value.

This reconciliation brings men back into the orbit of fellowship with God. By our sins, we place ourselves outside of God's family, and yet He forgives us and by His love He draws us back to Him.

We cannot come back by our own power; we have to wait for Him to receive us. When we have faith in the God of Jesus Christ, our separation from God and from other people is healed. So Christian salvation begins. This is the turning point of the drama of Redemption, as it is the turning point of all history. "God was in Christ reconciling the world to himself."

Act IV brings us the Church. Out of the work of God in Christ there came something new in the life of men. It is the new kind of group life in which Christian relationships exist. This change in men's relations to God and to each other began with Pentecost, when the experience of God as Holy Spirit brought three thousand people into the Christian fellowship through Baptism. This group is the Church.

So we are baptized and enter the dynamic fellowship of Christian love. Baptism is not only a social ceremony which brings the family together. Baptism is the means whereby God accepts a child as His child, and thus acts through the parents to bring the child into a redeemed and redemptive fellowship.

Through the new relationships in the Church, we come to know ourselves for what we are—sinners, who like lost sheep have strayed from God who is the Good Shepherd and who have become reconciled with God through His love for us. The power of God's Spirit assists us to become obedient servants of the heavenly Father.

Act V is the Consummation. This is the end of the drama. It is here, and yet it is not here. It tells us that God is judging us *now,* and that God will judge us when we die. It tells us that God stands above and beyond all history as the timeless Judge. It is either the promise of an eternal relationship with God, which is what heaven is, or it is the promise of eternal separation from God, which is what hell is. We have the choice! The end of the drama for each of us is doubtful until we make the decision which He offers us.

By these five acts of the drama—Creation, Covenant, Christ,

Church, and Consummation—God has entered the historical process to save us from sin and separation, from loneliness and frustration, from sickness and death. This is the good news of redemption, by which we are drawn from our own selfish ways to a life of the service of God.

II.

Perhaps the Christian Gospel was not presented to you in this way when you went to Sunday school, but this is the heart of the Gospel, and we need to educate each individual in the true and saving knowledge of Christ. It is not a matter for the church school alone, but involves each and every member of the Church.

The gospel of "redemption is learned by sharing in the redeeming relationships within a truly Christian home and within the life of a truly Christian parish family. The real job of Christian education is to help our families create the relationships of a truly Christian home and the leaders of parishes to create truly Christian relationships among its members. By living and sharing in these Christian relationships day by day, year by year, children and adults find religion meaningful and the help it gives them real."[1] "The Church exists for the purpose of re-enacting the Gospel story. Here, in the Christian family and parish life, the divine love which accepts the unlovable and unworthy becomes a reality in experience, since the Christ of the Cross is here a continuing presence and power."[2]

This position is the essence of the educational philosophy of the Protestant Episcopal Church and is to be discovered in the source materials of its new series of lessons. It is *education for Redemption.* It confronts our teachers, parents, and members with some basic questions.

---

[1] *Toward the Redemptive Life* (Leadership Training Pamphlet of the Protestant Episcopal Church), p. 14.

[2] Theodore Wedel, *World Christian Education* (Autumn 1952), p. 31.

The teachers need to ask themselves: "To what extent does today's lesson lead to a greater appreciation of God's mighty acts in the drama of Redemption, and how does this apply to the lives of my pupils? To what extent does the group experience of my class act as a way of redemption for its members? Is my teaching a ministry of reconciliation whereby my pupils are confronted with their Redeemer?"

It is equally a question for parents. In the home and community, there are many opportunities for redemptive fellowship. They need to ask themselves: "Is the atmosphere of our home such that our children know themselves to be loved and accepted? Are we mediators of God's love as expressed in discipline, forgiving love, guidance, and outreach? Is our home a community of redemptive love?"

Finally, it confronts all of us, as we ask ourselves: "How far do we enter into the redemptive fellowship of the Church's life? Do we know why we worship? Do we know what Christ has done for us? Do we expose ourselves to the sources of power by which our lives are renewed and we become true servants of our Father in heaven? Or are we content to stay outside, and in our loneliness and frustration continue to live a life of hell—of separation from God?"

Remember the words written to Timothy: "In the presence of God and of Jesus Christ who will judge the living and dead, in the light of his appearance and his reign, I adjure you to preach the word; keep at it in season and out of season, refuting, checking, and exhorting men; never lose patience with them, and never give up your teaching." (II Tim. 4:1-2, M)

Christian education for redemption is an everyday task for every person. Remember the rule given to Jewish parents: There is only one God, and you must love the Lord your God with all your mind, and all your soul, and all your strength. "These words you must learn by heart, this charge of mine. You must impress them on your children, you must talk about them when you are sitting at home and when you are on the road, when you lie down and when you rise up. You must tie them on your hands as a momento, and wear them on your forehead as a badge; you must inscribe them on the door-posts of your houses and on your gates." (Deut. 6:6-9, M)

Education for Redemption must go on among us at all times. For everyone must know the good news of the saving knowledge of Jesus Christ, and it is up to us to carry the story of the mighty acts of God in the drama of Redemption to all the people in our midst.

3.

GOD PLUS MAN!

THIRD SUNDAY IN ADVENT

PSALM 85; ISAIAH 35; LUKE 1:57-72; HYMNS 544, 521, 522, 518

World minus God equals nothing:
God minus world equals God.

This equation comes from Archbishop William Temple. It is the recognition of our total dependence on God and of God's independence of us. Schleiermacher put the center of religion here when he said that religion is the feeling of "absolute dependence on God."

There are many who lack this sense of dependence on God. They are like little Ellen who went to Jean's house for dinner. When Jean's father bowed his head and said something, Ellen asked what had been said. Jean replied:

"Daddy said grace."

"What's grace?" asked Ellen.

"It's thanking God for our food."

To which Ellen exclaimed, "Oh! we pay for ours."[1]

Johnny ran into a similar situation in reverse. He went to a home where everyone sat down and began to eat, and he asked: "Don't you say a prayer before you eat?"

The reply was, "No, we don't take time for that."

---

[1] Quoted in *Encyclopedia of Wit, Humor and Wisdom,* compiled and edited by Leewin B. Williams (Nashville: Abingdon-Cokesbury), No. 2882. Used by permission of the publisher.

The boy thought for a moment and then said, "You're just like my dog. You start right in."[2]

So far as we know, animals have no sense of dependence upon the divine. They do not know who they are or what their destiny is; thus, they act as if there is no God.

For some of us, this is a world in which God is not real, or at least He is like an absentee landlord. Perhaps we think of God as a child thought of his mother when he prayed:

> "Bless the dear clinic which weighed me with care,
> And the nursery-school teacher who tooth-combed my hair,
> And the youth-movement leaders, so care-worn for me,
> And my mother, God bless her, whom I never see."[3]

I.

Dr. Temple's equation is much profounder than these childhood illustrations. When he writes that

"world minus God equals nothing,"

he means that God created the world and holds it together, and that if God ever withdrew from the world, there would be no world. The importance of saying God created the world is not that He started this process at the beginning of time, but that the world is held together by His conscious will at every moment. The world continues to exist only because God wills it. God's nature is to be continually creative.

If we go back in history, to the time when our universe was in a prehistoric state, "it is surely quite clear that if anyone studied the world before there was life on it, he could never have predicted life; if he had studied vegetation, he would never have predicted animal life; if he had studied the animal world, he would never

---

[2] *Ibid.,* No. 2889.
[3] *Ibid.,* No. 2895.

have predicted human civilization and the arts; and if he had studied the selfishness of mankind, he could never have predicted a life of perfect and selfless love. At each stage, we reasonably trace the special activity of the will whose purpose is the explanation of all things."[4]

We sometimes use as a slogan during the summer months, "If God took a vacation, where would you be?" It is as simple as that. We are dependent on God "for our creation, preservation, and all the blessings of this life."

II.

The second part of Temple's equation is equally profound:

"God minus world equals God."

In a day when we are not sure that the world will continue to exist, it is reassuring to know that God does not depend on this world for His existence. Once, when discussing the significance of the atomic bomb for religion, Professor Hugh Vernon White said: "If an atomic chain reaction destroyed the world, there would still be God."

If Dr. White's statement is to be reassuring, I suppose it depends on how much faith we have. Is it any satisfaction to the survivors of Hiroshima or Nagasaki to be told that God is still God? Kiyoshi Tanimoto lived through the blast and is now at work on the Hiroshima Peace Foundation, with deeper faith in God than before the war. I think it is a great satisfaction to know that God cannot be destroyed.

Whether we are faced with a cataclysm or with a scientific view of the universe, we know that this earth can last only so long. There is a running down of the earth's energy, and sooner or later there

---

[4] *Daily Readings from William Temple* (London, Hodder and Stoughton), No. 404. Used by permission.

will be a noninhabitable earth. Or it may come from an explosion of the sun. Furthermore, and here we are certain of what will happen, life on this earth ends for each of us.

This statement by Dr. Temple is profound, whether we are in the midst of tragedy of a catastrophic nature, or whether we are sailing along in a universe that is slowly running down. This is God's world, and He will continue to be God after we and our world are gone. For we are God's, and thus we will not really be gone.

So we see that Dr. Temple's equation is really incomplete. It is true as far as it goes, but it does not face the positive question. What happens when we change our problem to:

God plus man?

III.

In this universe that God has made and continually holds together, there is that strangest of all animals: man. Man has a special place in God's plan. We all recognize this difference. G. K. Chesterton used to say, "No one asks a puppy what kind of dog it means to be when it grows up." [5] Puppies do not choose ends; man does. And man's chief end is "to glorify God and enjoy Him forever."

It is possible to think of man minus God, but we discover that this is nothing. It is possible to think of God minus man, and God will still be God. But when we change the equation to God plus man, we see that it makes a difference to God and makes all the difference to man.

Man is intended for fellowship with the eternal God. Therefore, man's behavior is of more than local or personal significance. Man has more value than an animal because God loves him. Dr. Temple puts it this way:

---

[5] William Temple, *The Church Looks Forward* (New York: Macmillan, 1944), p. 82.

"If I am a creature with a life-span of sixty or seventy years, I cannot count for anything over against the nation or the State. But if I am a child of God, destined for eternal fellowship with him, I have therein a dignity with which the State can make no comparable claim. . . . In the English Coronation service the King is seated as the token of earthly royalty is placed upon his head, but he is kneeling when just afterwards he receives the effectual tokens of divine grace in the same manner in which any laborer in any village church receives them." [6]

"God plus man," therefore, is the key to understanding the present situation, for we know the other equations lead to nothingness for us or to God's separation from His creation.

"World minus God equals nothing" is a philosophy of nihilism, of meaningless activity with no sense of the ultimate value of man. It is expressed in various ways in Communism, Fascism, and American materialism.

"God minus world equals God" is a profound challenge to those who worship the things of this world. It says that no evil is strong enough to destroy God. While we are dependent on God for our existence, God does not depend on us.

Yet God is not satisfied with this, for He has made the world for a purpose. He has not set up man as a toy, to be destroyed whenever the proper time comes. He is working out his purpose in history, and by sending His Son to redeem man, He made us take history seriously.

Thus, we are face to face with the third equation:

"God plus man equals God's kingdom."

When men are obedient to God and seek to do His will, then is God's kingdom among us. "For where two or three are gathered in

---

[6] *Ibid.*, pp. 82-83.

my name, there am I in the midst of them." (Matt. 18:20, RSV) "The kingdom of God is in the midst of you." (Luke 17:21, RSV)

IV.

God is among us today. It is upon Him that we are absolutely dependent for "our creation, preservation, and all the blessings of this life." As we face God in our midst, the words of the Litany are particularly appropriate:

"Remember not, Lord, our offences, nor the offences of our forefathers; neither take thou vengeance of our sins: Spare us, good Lord, spare thy people, whom thou hast redeemed with thy most precious blood, and be not angry with us for ever."

The words of Chesterton's hymn strike close to home:

> "O God of earth and altar,
> Bow down and hear our cry,
> Our earthly rulers falter,
> Our people drift and die." (Hymn 521)

Throughout the Old Testament, God is pictured against the background of a people besieged by their enemies. The prophets spoke to their times, and Isaiah proclaimed faith in Yahweh when the security of Israel was threatened. But Israel was overrun, and the people were taken captive. Out of the experience of being displaced persons in Babylon, however, came the teaching of the unknown prophet who wrote the latter part of Isaiah, telling them, "Comfort, comfort my people." Only through suffering could salvation come. There would be a Messiah and Israel would be the suffering servant.

Israel needed to learn that their loyalty must be to God Himself, that this is God's world, and that God would act in time to redeem history. The answer lies in the equation of God plus man, which means that we are members of God's kingdom as well as citizens of American democracy. It is our task to make this world a province of God's kingdom, as Toynbee has said, but it is more important that our primary citizenship be higher than the kingdoms of this world.

Robert Elliott Fitch summarizes this brilliantly in his *Kingdom Without End:* "Where, then, lies man's true glory? Is it not that he should be a citizen of the kingdom without end? Is it not that he should delight in those things in which God delights? Our true glory is not in the pride of power, nor in the pride of possessions, nor in the pride of intellect, nor in spiritual pride. Nor is our glory in ourselves and in our own virtue. Our glory is in God, that we know him, that we understand that it is he who exercises on earth the justice and the loving-kindness and the righteousness in which he takes delight. It is our glory, also, that, though we fall short of perfection, we may have a share in his justice and loving-kindness and righteousness; and that, being made in the image of the creator God, we, too, have a part in the creation of whatsoever is true and honest and lovely and of good report in this life. So may we march in the battalions and wave the banners of the kingdom without end." [7]

> "World minus God equals nothing."
> "God minus world equals God."
> "God plus man equals the kingdom without end."

---

[7] Robert Elliott Fitch, *Kingdom Without End* (New York: Scribners), p. 126. Used by permission of the publisher.

4.

"LET EV'RY HOUSE BE BRIGHT!"

CHRISTMAS

PSALM 89:1-30; ISAIAH 9:2-7; LUKE 2:1-20; HYMNS 21, 14, 33, 27

Christmas, when seen from a Christian perspective, has tremendous significance for every man. It is the beginning of the hope of the world. Surely there is no hope without the message of Christmas.

Howard Chandler Robbins wrote a Christmas hymn that begins with Christ enthroned in glory. It then turns to the child in the manger, but sees Him as sent by God and as returned to God. Christmas, then, is an act of God's love. We are not here simply to meditate about the birth of a Jewish baby. We are here to worship God and to give thanks for his gift of Jesus Christ, who came and died and rose again that this world might be saved from its sins. A little boy put it right when he said, "If we didn't have Easter, we couldn't have Christmas either."

"Now yield we thanks and praise
To Christ enthroned in glory." (Hymn 14)

This is the beginning of the story of redemption. It is through the work—the birth, life, death, and Resurrection—of Jesus Christ, that God became reconciled to the world and the world to Him. Christmas is an act of God for the sake of men.

"And on this day of days
Tell out redemption's story." (Hymn 14)

I.

What, then, is Christmas? It is our celebration of Jesus' birth. Jesus was born probably in the spring of 4 or 6 B.C. The wonderful stories surrounding His birth in Bethlehem are significant not because of how He was born or where, but because they tell us that "to you is born this day in the city of David a Savior, who is Christ the Lord." (Luke 2:11, RSV) The significant fact about Bethlehem's babe is that God sent Him. He came as a saviour, to redeem men from their sins. So we sing, "O come, let us adore him, Christ the Lord." (Hymn 12)

This is no purely personal event, involving Mary and Joseph. The vivid imagery of angels, stars, shepherds, and astrologers is to show that this birth has cosmic significance. This is a world-shaking event. This is the turning point in history—in the history of the world—but even more in your history and mine.

When you and I face up to this particular Christmas, we are not remembering a baby asleep on the hay. We are remembering One who came and lived and died that you and I might have eternal life. The Jesus Christ whom we remember, we also worship. He can be with us now, as the living Lord, if we will let Him. It is no simple poetic phrase when we sing:

> "O holy child of Bethlehem!
> Descend to us, we pray;
> Cast out our sin, and enter in,
> Be born in us today." (Hymn 21)

This response to the Redeemer, born once upon a time in a Palestine stable and born again in us, is the crucial decision of Christmas.

II.

So we say, "Christ is here." We repeat it as if to reassure ourselves, for we are not sure. We sing,

"Yet with the woes of sin and strife
The world has suffered long;
Beneath the heavenly strain have rolled
Two thousand years of wrong;
And man, at war with man, hears not
The tidings which they bring;
O hush the noise, ye men of strife,
And hear the angels sing!" (Hymn 19, stanza 3)

There is nothing of The Timid Soul about this kind of faith. This is not simply a festival for worshiping a pretty baby. Christian faith has always discarded both Pollyanna and Caesar. Realism about the nature of man has been its guiding light in the analysis of our human predicament. Christ calls sinners to repentance, not to happiness overnight.

"Child, for us sinners
Poor and in a manger,
We would embrace thee . . ." (Hymn 12, stanza 5)

The radical insight of Christian faith into the nature of man is the starting point of every Christmas celebration. Studdert-Kennedy put his finger on the sore spot of every Christian's self-analysis when he wrote, in the dialect of the English cockney:

"There's nothin' in man that's perfect,
And nothin' that's all complete,
'E's nubbat a big beginnin'
From 'is 'ead to the soles of 'is feet.
There's summat as draws 'im uppards,
And summat as drags 'im dahn,
An' the consekence is as 'e wobbles,
Twixt muck and a golden crahn.
An' it's just the same wi' the nations

As it is wi' a single man,
There's 'eaven and 'ell in their vitals,
A scrappin' as 'ard as they can." [1]

To men such as these and to nations such as these, Christmas is the promise of "peace to men of good will, peace to the men God favors, men that are God's friends, in whom God is well pleased." (Luke 2:14) For God in Christ will change us, will transform us, will respond to our faith with His wonderful gifts of grace; and because we are remolded in His way we will be obedient sons of the heavenly Father.

Christmas is the good news that we have a Saviour! It is the living Christ who

"... on this day of days
Tells out redemption's story!"

God has entered the lists of history, so that the world might be reconciled to Him. Christ is here, now, in the midst of this congregation, among those who worship Him, among those who are gathered in His name. And the power of Christ can change you so that you will receive the peace which comes to "men that are God's friends."

III.

Now if this is what Christmas is all about, when stripped of the tinsel and romance and myth, then we are up against a great question:

"What tribute shall we pay
To him who came in weakness,
And in a manger lay
To teach his people meekness?" (Hymn 14)

---

[1] G. A. Studdert-Kennedy, *The Warrior, the Woman and the Christ* (New York: Harper), pp. 180-181. Used by permission of the publisher.

Perhaps you are familiar with the legend of the shepherd maiden. As she watched the Magi place their rich gifts at the baby's feet, she was sad because she had no offering. She did not dare to enter the stable. And as she stood in the cold snow, an angel saw her distress. The snow melted at her feet, perhaps from the warmth of her tears, and a small bush of winter roses grew in front of her as she watched. She took the roses, went inside, and worshiped the new-born King.

The important response, whether it was that of the wise men or of the shepherds, was that *they worshiped Him.* The tribute is always "our selves, our souls and bodies," which we offer to Him as "a reasonable, holy, and living sacrifice." There is no other tribute that is enough.

IV.

The result of this kind of Christmas tribute is shown in our lives.

"Let ev'ry house be bright;
Let praises never cease.
With mercies infinite
Our Christ hath brought us peace." (Hymn 14)

The message of Christmas finds its fulfilment in the home—"Let ev'ry house be bright." In the home, as elsewhere, the significance of Christmas is a matter of tribute to the Christ. Just as it does not matter whether the Magi bring rich gifts or the shepherd maiden brings winter roses, the value of a Christmas present is not significant in itself. The tribute that a man shows his wife at Christmas is a reflection of his love and loyalty throughout all the days of the year. A house is bright when the spirit of Christ is present among all its members, and sometimes a house is bright when one member of the household catches the secret and passes it on to his unsuspecting family.

V.

Christmas involves a babe in a manger. Christmas is a children's festival. But the baby and the children are significant only because Christmas is the feast of the Incarnation, when the Word became flesh and dwelt among us. It is more than flashing stars and heavenly choruses, for the star and the angels tell us the same thing: "Behold, I bring you good tidings of great joy, which shall be to all people. For unto you is born this day in the city of David a Saviour, which is Christ the Lord." (Luke 2:10-11, KJ)

"Let ev'ry house be bright!"

5.

GOD AND THE ASTROLOGERS

EPIPHANY

PSALM 46; ISAIAH 60:1-9; MATTHEW 2:1-12; HYMNS 49, 46, 51, 258

> There came wise men from the east. (Matt. 2:1, KJ)

The Latin word *magi* was translated wise men by Tyndale in 1525. Wyclif had used *kynges* (or wise men) in the first English Bible of 1382. It has been variously translated since as magians, magicians, and astrologers. It is the word from which comes our English word magic. The Greek means a Persian Magus, a magician or astrologer.

Wyclif had called them kynges (or wise men) reflecting the prophecy in the second Isaiah which reads:

> But upon you the Lord shall rise, . . .
> And kings by the brightness of your rising. . . .
> Gold and frankincense shall they bring. (Isa. 60:2b, 3b, 6b, G)

In the later versions of the Gospel stories there were three kings named Gaspar, Melchior, and Baltasar. But Matthew seems to mean simply that there were astrologers from the east. Their great concern about the stars indicates that they were astrologers rather than magicians, which are the only two possible translations of the word Magi.

I.

In the days before astronomy, astrology was respected. There were astrologers at every court. "The ancient Greek readers of Matthew understood this passage to mean that astrology bowed at the Messiah's cradle, acknowledging that its day was done." [1]

In ancient times, people believed that the stars in their courses determined human events. Frequently, astrologers were intelligent men who could prophesy the future with a degree of accuracy.

It is said that an astrologer once foretold the death of a lady whom Louis XI loved. He was called before the king, who intended to punish him, and asked if he could foretell his own fate. The astrologer answered that he would die three days before the king. The king believed him and took special pains to preserve the astrologer's life. This astrologer, however, was living by his wits, not by the stars. He was a better psychologist than astrologer.

Adolf Hitler was also said to have consulted with astrologers. A certain astrologer was asked when Hitler would die. The answer was that Hitler would die on a Jewish holiday. But the astrologer could not tell him which one, because, he said, any day that Hitler died would be a Jewish holiday.

II.

Christianity rejects astrology because it offers something better: "The heavens declare the glory of God; and the firmament showeth his handy-work." (Ps. 19:1, PB) The stars reveal to us the nature of God. The stars do not tell us about man. They tell us about God. The God who created the stars is a God of order, of harmony, of natural law. He created a dependable universe, in which the prophecy of future events depends on man's relation to God.

---

[1] Edgar J. Goodspeed, *Problems of New Testament Translation* (Chicago: Univ. Chicago Press), pp. 14-15.

This God who is revealed in terms of law and order, of the science of astronomy rather than the magic of astrology, is also given to us in historical events. The light of the star which led the astrologers to Bethlehem was replaced by the Light of the world. They no longer relied on the stars, but placed themselves in the service of their new Lord. They must have felt much like the old man, Simeon, who responded to the birth of Christ with the *Nunc Dimittis:*

> "Now, Master, thou canst let thy servant go, and go in peace,
> as thou didst promise;
> for mine eyes have seen thy saving power
> which thou hast prepared before the face of all the peoples,
> to be a light of revelation for the Gentiles,
> and a glory to thy people Israel." (Luke 2:29-32, M)

There is a light to lighten the heathen. In the fourth Gospel, Jesus says, "I am the light of the world; he who follows me will not walk in darkness, but will have the light of life." (John 8:12, RSV)

III.

On the narrow streets of Cairo, an Englishman, by the name of Temple Gairdner, used to ride a bicycle, charging in and out among the donkeys and camels. He worked among the Moslems: preached, wrote, and published in Arabic; edited a journal to promote understanding between Moslems and Christians; and was a student of native Egyptian and Syrian music. He worked there for thirty years—doing administrative work that he hated, teaching the lower grades in school, filling in where he was needed when other men got tired and went home. "Man!" he said once to a friend, "the only thing in the world worth living for is to find out the will of God and do it." A church was erected in his memory called—The Church of the Light of the World.

This same spirit of loyalty was evident in Hudson Stuck. Mount Denali (the great one) is the Indian name for Mount McKinley, It is over twenty thousand feet high and is a challenge to any mountain climber. For nearly fifty years men were turned back as they attempted to break the spell of this champion of North American mountains. Then came the man who succeeded. He spent ten years planning, hoping, and dreaming, as he traveled over Alaska by dog-sled and river boat. After eleven weeks of climbing and camping in the bitter cold, Hudson Stuck and his three companions finally made it. This man was a missionary, the archdeacon of the Yukon. *The New York Times* reviewed his book, *Ascent of Denali,* and said, "It makes one wish that all mountain climbers might be archdeacons." In the same courageous way, Stuck fought for his Eskimos when the canneries threatened their fish supply, when they were sick, and when they needed any kind of help. He saw the light, and brought it to the land of the northern light. Today his name lives in The Hudson Stuck Memorial Hospital.

These men lived beyond their normal resources because they were guided by the Light of the world. They saw that

> "Christ is the world's true Light,
> Its Captain of salvation,
> The Day-star clear and bright
> Of every man and nation." (Hymn 258)

IV.

There are times of darkness, when the light seems to be out. There was a time when men did not know how to obtain light from electricity; there was a time when there were no candles; there was a time when men went to bed with the setting of the sun. But just as the resources for piercing the physical darkness were always present, so the resources of spiritual light are available for the asking. We can take our own light with us wherever we go.

We can face inconveniences; we can face the loss of seeming necessities; we can accept the absence of essentials; we can even become reconciled to the death of our friends and loved ones, because we have our own light in us. It is the light of the power of God which never fails us.

Jesus on the cross saw darkness for a moment: "Why hast thou forsaken me?" "It is finished." But it is not finished, and He cries, "Father, into thy hands I commend my spirit." And that is the *end of the beginning* rather than the beginning of the end. The light flickers in the vacillating soul of the thrice-denying Peter. A flame glows and catches fire. Others begin to see the light. Like a consuming flame they are overtaken by the spirit, and the Church of the Light of the World is born.

The first letter of John makes this clear:

> "This is the message that we heard from him and announce to you: God is light; there is no darkness in him at all. If we say, 'We have fellowship with him,' and yet live in darkness, we are lying and not living the truth. But if we live in the light, just as he is in the light, we have fellowship with one another, and the blood of Jesus his Son cleanses us from every sin" (I John 1:5-7, G)

The light has not gone out. If an individual can have a church named after him (The Church of the Light of the World); if an archdeacon can climb Denali and serve the people of Alaska; if men can carry the Light of the glory of God to the ends of the world, then there is hope for each one of us. The stars in their courses do not determine the destiny of men; astrology has given way to the Light born in a manger; and the story of Epiphany is that "God is light; there is no darkness in him at all."

Dwight Bradley has written some words which fit us today:

"We hear it said that the lights have gone out, in Europe, in the world.

Such a thing has happened many times before.
It was dark in Bethlehem on a certain night,
Yet on that night a new star was shining.
Shepherds looked up and saw a glory in the sky; saw a glowing radiance around a mother and her child.

"The lights had gone out then, in Judea, in Rome.
Yet it was bright enough to guide three wise men on their way towards truth,
Bright enough to rouse the shepherds to the coming of a prince of peace,
Bright enough to fill a cattle shed where human hope was born.

"There is light enough today to make a track of thought for those who have a mind to hunt for living truth,
Enough to show the peoples of the earth the way to build a democratic world in justice and good will,
Enough to fill with understanding and with courage any room, hall, meeting house, or open square,
Where men and women plan good things for the human race.

"There is light enough for all these things.

"What if old lights have gone out?
Kindle new ones everywhere,
Get out your lamp, your candle, or your lantern.
Put it in a window, or better still—
Take your own light with you and go outdoors into the world.
You will be surprised to find so many there ahead of you.
You may be even more surprised to find that God, himself, is there with his newest and brightest star!" [2]

---

[2] From *Social Action,* Dec. 15, 1940. Published by the Council for Social Action of the Congregational Christian Churches and used by permission of the author, Dwight Bradley.

6.

"NOT AS ONE THAT BEATETH THE AIR"

SEPTUAGESIMA

PSALM 121; JOSHUA 1:1-9; I CORINTHIANS 9:24-27; HYMNS 577, 576, 572, 560

> So fight I, not as one that beateth the air. (I Cor. 9:26a, KJ)
>
> I am no shadow-boxer; I really fight. (P)

In this remarkable passage, Paul reveals the qualities of a boxing or track coach. He had a vigorous and vital faith, and he knew how to tell others about it. This is the day when we sing such hymns as "Awake, my soul, stretch every nerve, and press with vigor on," "Fight the good fight with all thy might," as we hear the Master say, "Go work today."

Beating the air is a popular pastime. A boxer often starts a wild haymaker from the floor, and it travels through the air with great force, hitting nothing. There is futility in this type of fighting, and the one who wastes his energy with wild blows eventually tires and loses the match.

Have you ever seen a housekeeper try to straighten the front room when the announcement is made that company will arrive in ten minutes? Here, there, everywhere she rushes, putting a pillow here, moving it there, putting it back again. She places newspapers on the mantel, takes them off and tosses them in the wastebasket, and then puts them on the reading table. Then the doorbell rings and, because she has wasted so much energy, nothing else has been touched. She has been running uncertainly and is exhausted.

So often we feel hurried. A man is late for dinner, and in his haste to dress on time, he drops a collar button from his jittery fingers and wastes five minutes looking for it under the dresser. There is the last minute discovery that a sock has not been darned, and so the needle goes through the sock and the thumb (if a man is doing it) or into the finger (if a woman is doing it), and time is wasted while the thumb or finger is covered with a bandage. Haste makes waste, and we beat the air.

I.

Paul also says that "our contest is for an eternal crown that will never fade." (P) In a physical contest, there is only one winner, while in the greater contest of the spirit in which all men are entered, there is an eternal reward.

This is the major point of the Gospel for today: Jesus tells a parable of the householder who pays all men the same wage no matter how long they have worked for him. This story is disturbing to those who see it in terms of earthly economics. But Jesus' parable has nothing to do with economics. It applies to the kingdom of God, with God as the householder. All men are children of God, and His grace applies equally to all men. God is not concerned with strict justice or sound economics at this point. There may be one-twelfth of a denarius or of a pound or of a dollar, but there is no such thing as one-twelfth of God's love. The point is that God's approval is completely nonlegal. A. E. Barnett writes, "There is inevitably wide difference between persons on any sort of achievement basis, but among those who within limits of ability and opportunity are utterly devoted to their tasks there is equality in the realm of spirit. The thing commended in the parable is this readiness of response to opportunity and a corresponding zeal for service thereafter. Whether opportunity came early or late, all answered wholeheartedly and labored earnestly."[1]

God does not demand uniformity of ability, but He demands purity of motive and spirit. So Paul and Jesus are saying the same thing. Only one can win a corruptible crown; only one can win a fading wreath; only one can get the worldly reward; but all may win the incorruptible crown. All may win the unfading wreath; all may win God's gift of love and happiness. In God's vineyard, human standards are reversed, and God's grace gives to all men who serve Him a crown that cannot be spoiled by moth or rust.

II.

Men do not always see this. Or seeing it, they refuse to accept it. They continue to beat the air with their efforts; they waste their energy. They are frustrated because they do not want to be subject to the householder who sends them into his vineyard.

But Paul saw it. In his second letter to the Corinthians, he is maneuvered into boasting of his achievements. These are athletic in nature, and yet they are in terms of his service to God. He lists the number of times he was imprisoned, beaten, shipwrecked, stoned; he was in danger from floods, bandits, and his own countrymen; and he had known hunger, thirst, cold, and lack of clothes. And when he was about to be arrested, he escaped by climbing through a window and being let down the wall in a basket.

"Polycarp, the venerable and renowned bishop of Smyrna," ran his race without swerving and was never in doubt as to his goal. He was arrested because he would not burn incense before the emperor and say that "Caesar is Lord." He was taken to the arena, and was offered another chance to renounce Christ. And he said:

[1] A. E. Barnett, *Understanding the Parables of Our Lord* (Nashville: Abingdon-Cokesbury), p. 188. Used by permission of the author.

> "For eighty-six years I have been his slave, and he has done me no wrong; how can I blaspheme my king who has saved me?"

The governor insisted that he swear by the fortune of Caesar, and he answered,

> "If you imagine that I will swear by the fortune of Caesar, as you say, and pretend not to know who I am, let me tell you plainly, I am a Christian. And if you want to learn the doctrine of Christianity, set a day and hear me."

When he was threatened with wild animals and fire, Polycarp rose to even greater heights,

> "You threaten me with the fire that burns for an hour and in a little while goes out, for you do not know about the fire of the coming judgment and everlasting punishment, which is reserved for the wicked. But why do you wait? Bring on whatever you please."

And when they were going to nail him down, he said,

> "Leave me as I am, for he who enables me to endure the fire will also enable me to stay on the pyre without moving, without your fastening me with nails."[2]

While most of us today do not have the opportunities for martyrdom that Paul and Polycarp had, it is not an impossibility. Dietrich Bonhoeffer was a young German Christian who was opposed to Hitler. He helped maintain an underground seminary to train ministers during the war; he kept in contact with the

---

[2] "Martyrdom of Polycarp," 8:2-12:1, 13:3, in Edgar J. Goodspeed, *The Apostolic Fathers* (New York: Harper), pp. 247-252. Used by permission of the publisher.

churches outside Germany through the World Council of Churches and flew to Sweden for a meeting; and he was instrumental in the plot of Christian leaders to destroy Hitler. Finally, he was put to death by the storm troopers without trial. The Norwegian Bishop Eivind Berggrav faced Vidkun Quisling with courage and poise, and when Quisling shouted, "You deserve to have your head chopped off," Berggrav replied calmly, "Well, here I am." He was imprisoned in a house during the Nazi occupation, but was in touch with all the underground forces. He wrote a book and kept himself alert to all that was going on around him. A peasant woman managed to get to him with a bottle of milk and told him how her husband had heard over the radio that the Archbishop of Canterbury was offering prayers for him.

III.

When we say we are Christians, do we give evidence of a vigorous and vital faith? Do we "stretch every nerve and press with vigor on?" Or are we like those who prefer shadow boxing, where we fight by beating the air? When the chips are down, do we play for keeps?

Paul and Polycarp, Bonhoeffer and Berggrav, and many in the interim believed that "Christ is thy strength and Christ thy right."

What have we done to spread the good news of Jesus Christ? Is there any connection between our faith and the missionary work of the Church in China, or Japan, or Latin America? Is there any connection between our faith and the influence we have on our pagan friends? Have we brought anyone into the Church? What is the relevance of our faith for our life with our families?

It is true that our fear of ridicule from our friends and families may be almost as great as Polycarp's fear of lions in the arena or the pyre of fire. And when we are afraid of ridicule, when we are afraid of life, when our frustrations and fears show up in beating the air, we need to remember Polycarp's words as they were going to nail him down: "Leave me as I am, for he who enables me to endure the fire will also enable me to stay on the pyre without moving, without your fastening me with nails."

Christian faith can rise to this level. The unfading wreath comes to us when we use what abilities God has given us in complete devotion to Him. We find the sources of power for this vigorous and vital faith in our worship, as we meet God in prayer and sacrament, in preaching, through hymns and psalms and the scripture. For then we are cleansed, uplifted, transformed. We literally feed upon the love of God, and this gives us the power to run the race, and not uncertainly, and to fight, but not as one that beateth the air.

Christian faith is the *plus* that makes life worthwhile. A knocking motor in an automobile will run more smoothly if it has the *plus* of ethyl gasoline, which conserves energy and puts its power to work. The *plus* of worship takes the energy potentially in us and gives it power and direction. The knocks of wasted energy and frustration are eliminated, and we turn our motives and aptitudes to single-hearted devotion to God's will. We still may not be worth very much in the eyes of the world, and we may still have to work for one-twelfth of a denarius, but in God's eyes we know that we are worth the full denarius if we have served Him with wholeness of mind and heart and soul.

Let us then, encouraged by the good examples of such saints as Paul and Polycarp, Bonhoeffer and Berggrav, persevere in running "the race that is set before us, looking unto Jesus the author and finisher of our faith; who for the joy that was set before him endured the cross, despising the shame, and is set down at the right hand of the throne of God." (Heb. 12:2, KJ)

7.

LENT AGAIN

ASH WEDNESDAY

PSALM 32; DEUTERONOMY 10:12-15, 17-11:1; I JOHN 2:1-17;

HYMNS 55, 61, 310, 336 (521 *for* LITANY)

[Lent almost always coincides with spring training for baseball players. The players gather in their various camps, located in warm climates. They start with running to loosen their muscles; then with care, they try throwing. They practice batting against easy throwers or even a mechanical pitcher. After about a month, they are in fine shape for the beginning of the season. This period of preparation is essential to good playing. Sometimes a player holds out for more money, misses spring training, and starts the season without this practice. As a result he must start slowly, and other players outplay him for the first few weeks. Even a star player cannot afford to miss spring practice.

So it is with Lent. It is the spring training period of religion. Only those who get in condition spiritually are fit to appreciate Easter, and it is they who give the most and get the most from the great climax of the Christian year. Others are not ready for it, and they see Easter (so to speak) from the grandstand without being real partakers.

Even an automobile needs occasional special service. Some people believe that regular refueling and adding oil is sufficient, but the car will not continue to run efficiently unless it gets special attention from time to time. There is lubrication to get rid of rattles and squeaks and to make the parts last longer; there is motor tuning to improve efficiency; there is the recharging of the battery.

Some of us mishandle our automobiles, and have squeaky, inefficient, and undependable cars. Many people treat themselves the same way spiritually. They come to church on Easter without having put themselves in condition; their knees literally crack from disuse; their emotional responses are inefficient; they have not recharged their spiritual batteries. To mix our metaphors, they are a combination of an athlete unprepared for strenuous competition in highly specialized play and an automobile which has been misused.

Lent, then, is a time for spiritual spring training, a time for lubricating our souls. It is a time for resetting the gap in our spiritual spark plugs. All of this is preparation for the climax of the Church year. How can you expect to share in the entry on Palm Sunday, in the Last Supper on Maundy Thursday, in the Crucifixion on Good Friday, and in the Resurrection on Easter, without adequate preparation?

I.

Jesus did not come to His mission unprepared. The forty days of Lent are based on the story of Jesus' forty days in the wilderness. He was tempted to misuse His power, and He needed to make explicit His own vocation as the one sent by God for a special task. The last week of Lent parallels Jesus' final preparation for His death. The whole drama from Palm Sunday to Good Friday is a pageant of preparation for the victory of the cross and the subsequent Resurrection. For us, also, Lent is a means of our preparation for sharing in the Resurrection power that comes from faith in Jesus as the Christ.

First, there is your relation to God: "for the LORD your God is the God of gods, and the Lord of lords, the great, mighty, and awful God, who is never partial, and never takes a bribe, who secures justice for the orphan and the widow, and loves the resident alien in giving him food and clothing." (Deut. 10:17, G)

Man's first loyalty is to God's will. Man's wholeness of being lies in God. Without God, man is nothing. Man drifts away from God, or treats Him in a commonplace manner, or believes that ritual is sufficient. Man fails to give of himself, and therefore God will do nothing for him.

"You shall therefore love the Lord your God, and keep his charge, his statutes, his ordinances, and his commandments always." (Deut. 11:1, RSV) "Whoever says, 'I know him,' but does not obey his commands, is a liar, and there is no truth in his heart." (I John 2:4, G)

So we come to our second task, which is the realization of our own failures. We have not fought the good fight and have not seen clearly what is the straight race. Christ has not been the path.

Lent is a time for the emphasis on acknowledgment of sin. It properly begins with the Penitential Office. Throughout the forty days, we are constantly reminded that there are things we ought not to have done, and there are things we have left undone which we ought to have done. "Weary of earth, and laden with my sin," as one of the old hymns puts it.

Repentance for individual and social sins is a sure sign of the health of the Church. It has been said that had the Church stressed its own guilt as it should, the world would not be as bad off as it is. The sin with which we are concerned involves us as individuals, but we need to recognize that we are members of communities which in their corporate nature disobey the will of God: the town in which we live, the state and the nation, the school, the corporation, and the Church. Involved as we are inextricably in the sins of mankind, we need help which only God can give.

Lent is a call to repentance, when we turn from our past way of life and seek the power of the Spirit to help us do better. As the psalmist puts it:

"How happy is he whose transgression is forgiven, whose sin is
covered!
How happy is the man to whom the Lord charges no guilt,
And in whose spirit there is no guile." (Ps 32:1-2, G)

Our third task is to seek forgiveness. "If anyone does sin, we have in Jesus Christ one who is upright and will intercede for us with the Father. He is himself an atoning sacrifice for our sins, and not only for ours but also for the whole world." (I John 2:1-2, G) The whole drama of Redemption centers in this faith as summarized by the man who was known simply as the "Elder." We do not always understand what faith in Christ means, but the experience of the ages tells us that when men have this faith their sins are washed away. Through what Christ did for us, we are able to appropriate to ourselves His power to cleanse and heal.

We do not always know our sins, but in every decision there are hidden motives of self-interest. We disguise our desires to give them seeming decency. We even fool ourselves. But what we think and feel and do does not escape God. "If we say we have no sin, we deceive ourselves, and the truth is not in us. If we confess our sins, he is faithful and just, and will forgive our sins and cleanse us from all unrighteousness. If we say we have not sinned, we make him a liar, and his word is not in us." (I John 1:8-10, RSV)

So we turn to God. We confess our sinful motives and actions. We seek to have in us the attitude that Jesus Christ had. This, then, is what Lent means: It is the special effort to be more devoted than ever before, more honest with ourselves and with God, and less centered in ourselves. This takes time and effort. Lent provides the opportunity, but we must make the best of every moment of it. And because we have prepared ourselves, the drama of the saving grace of God through the Easter story, re-enacted, can enter into our souls.

II.

Let us remember that Lent is a time for training and preparation. We must not exhaust our Lenten emotions on Ash Wednesday and then try to catch up hurriedly on Good Friday. We should decide what we are going to do about this Lent now, and then stick to it. It is wise to start slowly and extend our practices each week. There are too many Ash Wednesday Christians who forget the Penitential Office the moment it has been said.

Throughout Lent, we should keep the climax in mind. We must remember that we cannot share the glory of Easter without having shared the events that lead up to it. Lent is an opportunity to review the life of Christ in the Gospels, sharing His experiences as far as we are able. As *The Symphony of the Christian Year* reaches the crescendo of Holy Week, we can be ready to understand what is happening. Holy Week is a drama with a perfect climax. There is no letdown. In worshipful imagination, we ride to Jerusalem with Jesus on Palm Sunday, we visit the temple with Him, we share in that great experience in the Upper Room, we see the ugliness and tragedy of the Crucifixion, and finally there is Easter with all its tremendous power.

We should set up a plan for increasing private devotions during Lent. There are special services in many churches but we cannot stop there. Devotions become like Salt Lake if they have no expression in action. Just as nothing can live in the Dead Sea because it has no outlet, so God does not live in a heart which does not express itself in action. We can find something extra to do in church, in the community, in the family, which will express our renewed devotion to God. We can give up some useless activity or habit, and put the time or money saved into meaningful work.

We should be instructed in the meaning of Christianity. The best devotional activity for many of us is reading. We can read some book which deals with the Christian answer to a confused world. We can try to find Christian solutions for our own dilemmas. We can join study groups or form one. And our studying must be expressed in sacrificial activity.

III.

"Lent again," we say. To some, it is a bore. We are like the lazy baseball player who hates spring training. We are like the indolent motorist who neglects his car. We are like the unhealthy man who is ineffective because he takes poor care of his body. "Lent again." "Spring training again." Or, as some children would say in the old days of the weekly bath, "Saturday night again."

Lent has a cleansing effect when it is properly followed. It takes effort to cast off the mantle of habit and routine. It takes effort to decide that going to church once a week, or less, is insufficient, and that more than this is demanded of the Christian.

But the climax is coming. Easter follows the next forty weekdays. We shall be lost in the rush if we are not ready. Now is the time to begin. "For you yourselves know well that the day of the Lord will come like a thief in the night." (I Thess. 5:2, RSV)

In our devotions, reading, and service to God and man, we remember that it is through faith in Jesus Christ that men find the true love of God. Jesus died at the hands of wicked men, and yet He lives forever in the hearts of men. Let us be sure that He is in our hearts.

8.

"RIDE ON—TO DIE!"

PALM SUNDAY

PSALM 24; ZECHARIAH 9:9-12; MATTHEW 27:1-54 *or* MARK 11:1-11;

HYMNS 62, 68, 432, 64

In the midst of all the pomp of Palm Sunday, we need to see the triumphal entry in terms of the sequence of events. One of the hymns gives us the picture:

> "Ride on! ride on in majesty!
> In lowly pomp ride on to die;
> Bow thy meek head to mortal pain,
> Then take, O God, thy power, and reign."
> (Hymn 64, stanza 5)

I.

We do not know what the crowds thought or even how big the group was that called out to Jesus as he rode into Jerusalem on the donkey. We may assume that here were pilgrims coming to the Holy City from all parts of the world, heading for their shrine for the feast of the Passover. It was a gala crowd, made up mostly of ignorant outlanders but also of intelligent and wealthy Jews. They hailed this man who was acting out a part by fulfilling an Old Testament prophecy about the Messiah, and they were good-natured about Him as they called out: "Hosanna! Blessed be he who comes in the name of the Lord! Blessed be the kingdom of our father David that is coming! Hosanna in the highest!" (Mark 11:9, RSV)

What were they thinking about as they called out to Jesus? Most of them probably were not thinking at all about the significance of what they saw. A few may have thought of Him as a budding revolutionary. Some may have seen in His act the fulfilment of Zechariah's prophecy. But all of them would have dismissed the event from their minds—except for the dramatic occurrences that followed.

II.

There were disciples and other followers of Jesus in the crowds, too. They must have been filled with exaltation! Now something was going to happen! Their beloved leader was going to assert His messiahship, and they were elated. It was this expectation of fulfilment that led to such tragic disillusionment only a few days later. They may have thought of Him as a political messiah about to change the setup of Israel's government, or they may have thought of Him as a prophet who was going to reform Israel's religion. They had high hopes for Jesus and for themselves.

III.

Concerning Jesus, this much is sure. He knew what He was doing. He was acting out a prophecy upon which He must have meditated for a long time. He knew what was needed to fulfil Zechariah's prophecy, and He knew that meekness and suffering were the clues to the meaning of Messiah. Whether He knew that death was certain is doubtful; for until the last He prayed that He would not have to die. But that He was ready to suffer any pain that was necessary is obvious from the riding on the ass:

> "Lo, your king comes to you;
> triumphant and victorious is he,

> humble and riding on an ass,
> on a colt the foal of an ass." (Zech. 9:9, RSV)

He must have hoped that His victory would be achieved without the cross, but the fact that the cross was highly probable did not deter Him. He was willing to ride on—to die.

IV.

From our perspective, we can see the stark tragedy of it all. The young Prince of Glory was staking everything on going to Jerusalem. He was in search of victory for Himself and for His cause, and at every turn He met the rigid opposition of those in high places. He never had a chance, for although the common people heard him gladly, He had no influence on the group who controlled the government. During the week following his ride on the ass, He was faced with one group after another; and finally He drove his opponents to desperate measures.

Convinced that Jesus was dangerous to the *status quo* of religion, His opponents resolved that He should be put to death. It was not expedient to do this in daylight, for the crowds might not stand for it, but if they caught Him at night, they could run the charges through before the pilgrims to the Passover knew what it was all about. So they found Him alone, with the assistance of Judas, and took Him off.

Everything moved with incredible swiftness in order to clear the way for the Passover. The relations between the priests and politicians were so smooth that there was no delay in getting a hearing before Pilate. There was no one to champion the Galilean prophet, called the King of the Jews. Certainly Peter was of no help. Every one of His human relations was broken. Except for His heavenly Father, He was solitary and alone, friendless, and without anyone to champion Him.

V.

"Ride on—to die!"

The hymn, "All glory, laud, and honor," had a quaint final stanza that was dropped in the seventeenth century. It went like this:

"Be thou, O Lord, the rider,
And we the little ass;
That to God's Holy City
Together we may pass."[1]

Perhaps this stanza is not without significance, for it points to the guidance which we need from Christ. Paul writes to the Philippians: "Let this mind be in you, which was also in Christ Jesus." (Phil. 2:5, KJ)

For what did Christ do? And Paul continues: "And being found in human form, he humbled himself and became obedient unto death, even death on a cross. *Therefore* God has highly exalted him and bestowed on him the name which is above every name, that at the name of Jesus every knee should bow, in heaven and on earth and under the earth, and every tongue confess that Jesus Christ is Lord, to the glory of God the Father!" (Phil. 2:8-11, RSV)

Simeon Stylites (Dr. Halford Luccock), writing in the *Christian Century,* compares modern Christians with those of an earlier day. I am afraid he is a bit sarcastic, and yet he is saying something of significance:

"A Modern Roll Call of Martyrs:

"There is Polycarp Brown, for instance, who came to the morning service once every three months, on fine Sundays, and stayed all through to the benediction. Hell's foundations tremble when shaken by devotion like that.

---

[1] *The Hymnal 1940 Companion,* p. 47.

"There is St. Teresa Robinson, who made pies four times a year for the Ladies' Aid suppers.

"There is Pierpont Morton, who increased his subscription to the church from $2 to $3 a Sunday, and was fittingly rewarded by another deduction from his income tax.

"There is Barnabas Cox, who with unvarying fidelity attended the Easter service and the annual meeting every year; and Demos Duval, who attended two Men's Club dinners and played end man in the minstrel show.

"There is Mrs. Boanerges Johnson, who during the fall and winter drove her two children seven blocks to Sunday school, called for them at 11 a.m., and drove them home again.

"Of such is the Kingdom of Heaven." [2]

VI.

There is a contradiction between the drama of Palm Sunday leading surely to the cross and the life of the Church today. Being a Christian today does not involve many risks, and in the Church we discover a sense of well-being, a lack of urgency, a failure to challenge people to be courageous and forthright. Perverse Christians sometimes get involved in heresy trials, extremists refuse to salute the flag and, along with conscientious objectors, may end up in jail. But there is no demand for martyrdom. It is too easy to be a Christian—receive Baptism and Confirmation, come to Communion. We even give prizes sometimes to children who attend Sunday school. In a world which may be falling apart, or may be blown to pieces, the Church often seems to be a buffer to protect us from reality.

I am not suggesting that we should seek martyrdom, but as we meditate upon those mighty acts by which our Lord was betrayed,

---

[2] Halford Luccock, "A Modern Roll Call of Martyrs," *Christian Century.*

crucified, and risen again for your sake and mine, we need to look carefully at ourselves.

First, let us take seriously what Simeon Stylites has to say, and not take any credit for the doing of our duty. Let us assume that every good Christian will attend church even when it rains or snows, that no other church activity is a substitute for worship, that there are reasons for giving other than income tax deductions, that parents need to do more than send or transport their children to church school. Let us not give ourselves credit for striving toward minimum standards. If a boy gets a "C" in a course in which he is capable of earning an "A," we do not say he is an adequate scholar. We do not give awards for inadequate and spasmodic efforts toward any goal.

Let us think of the sure and certain steps that Jesus took after He dismounted from the messianic donkey. How do they compare with the uncertain steps we take toward His kingdom?

A second suggestion that stems from the Palm Sunday story is that Christianity is not tiddlywinks. It is a matter of life and death, of the eternal life of the soul, of the difference between damnation and salvation, of communion with Almighty God or absorption in one's own ego. In the Holy Week story there are many climaxes that remind us of the seriousness of our faith.

There is the decision in Gethsemane, when Jesus wants to be released from the serious business of facing death. And there is His thoroughly predictable response: "Not my will, but thine be done!" The trouble with every person on Simeon Stylites' list is that each one is a sinner who is cheerfully following his own motives and will, and then taking credit for it as if it were God's will. This is hypocrisy of a high order; possible only when people have been exposed to the Christian faith and it has not taken hold of them. Let us not fool ourselves into thinking we are doing what

God wants when all we have done is to draw a halo around our own desires.

In the third place, there is the fellowship of Holy Week. Table fellowship is the deepest kind of companionship, and it reaches the highest level in all history at the Last Supper. When you and I receive Holy Communion on Maundy Thursday, we will be reflecting on how the events of the final week of Jesus' life culminated in this last fellowship meal with His disciples. And our Easter Communion will reflect Jesus' victory as He comes to us as the Risen Christ. We come to the Lord's Table because it is His supper and He is host to us. He is truly present in the hearts of the faithful, of those who seek to do His will.

It is *for us* that Jesus Christ humbled Himself and became obedient even unto death. So we confess that Jesus Christ is Lord. By this confession of faith, our lives are changed, and we also become obedient children of the heavenly Father.

Let us take one final look at the last stanza of the hymn that describes what Jesus did for us on Palm Sunday:

"Ride on! ride on in majesty!
In lowly pomp ride on—to die; (for us!)
Bow thy meek head to mortal pain,
Then take, O God, thy power, and reign." (in us!) (Hymn 64)

9.

THE SACRAMENTAL MEANING OF THE CROSS

MAUNDY THURSDAY

I CORINTHIANS 11:23-26; LUKE 23:1-49

or PSALM 116; JEREMIAH 31:31-34; I CORINTHIANS 11:23-26;

HYMNS 199, 190, 191, 201

The cross is at the center of the Lord's Supper.

"All glory be to thee, Almighty God, our heavenly Father, for that thou, of thy tender mercy, didst give thine only Son Jesus Christ to suffer death upon the Cross for our redemption."[1] These are the opening words of the prayer of consecration at Holy Communion. They recall to us the centrality of the cross in our worship, the place of the cross in God's plan of salvation, and the power of the cross to save us.

We are to have a "perpetual memory of his precious death and sacrifice." "For in the night in which he was betrayed, he took Bread; and when he had given thanks, he brake it, and gave it to his disciples, saying, Take, eat, this is my Body, which is given for you; Do this in remembrance of me. Likewise, after supper, he took the Cup; and when he had given thanks, he gave it to them, saying, Drink ye all of this; for this is my Blood of the New Testament, which is shed for you, and for many, for the remission of sins; Do this, as oft as ye shall drink it, in remembrance of me."[2]

---

[1] Book of Common Prayer, p. 80.

[2] *Loc. cit.*, cf. I Cor. 11:23-25 in any modern translation.

We know that Christ is present in the Holy Communion, and we need also to see that the cross which is held in our memories at each Lord's Supper is sacramental in nature. The cross is "an outward and visible sign" of God's love for us. "So God loved the world, that he gave his only begotten Son, that whosoever should believe in him, should not perish, but have everlasting life." (John 3:16, PB)

The cross was the act that sealed the agreement between God and man. It certified God's love for man, making it clear that God would keep His word, for His promise was signed in blood. "This is my blood which ratifies the agreement, and is to be poured out for many people." (Mark 14:24, G) The cup stands for signing an agreement in blood. It is God's sacrificial offering of His Son for the sake of men.

In order to understand this agreement or covenant, we need to remember that it came at the end of a long relationship between God and man. In the Old Testament, Yahweh's first important covenant was the Ten Commandments, written in stone, providing a legal relationship with his people. Yahweh would keep His side of the agreement if the people would keep theirs. But Israel failed to keep the law, and the prophets promised judgment upon Israel for her sins. Then came a variation of the agreement, written on men's hearts when Jeremiah promised that God would write His law inwardly. The law was personalized, and still men rejected the Lord. So it took a new covenant, written in blood which stood for the sacrifice of God's only begotten Son, to provide the means where God was reconciling the world to Himself. It is this that we remember in the Holy Communion and in the life of the Church's worship and praise, for we take the bread and wine, "having in remembrance his blessed passion and precious death, his mighty resurrection and glorious ascension." It is the true meaning of Christian faith to trust in God who redeemed the world by His own act in Christ.

I.

As we think particularly of the Last Supper, we do not know how much of this deeper meaning was in the minds of the disciples. We cannot even conjecture what was going through the mind of Jesus, or how much He knew of the cosmic significance of the event. This was the last of a long series of meals that He had had with His disciples. If He had thought about the possibilities of loyal service on the part of His followers, there may have been some questions in His mind, perhaps like these:

How about Peter? Can he stand the temptations of the trial and death and disgrace? Peter will probably deny Me as the result of despair, but he will come through in the end.

And then there is John. He is sweet-souled and may be influential with some groups. He is noisy at times, as is his brother, James. John may become a pillar among the twelve, as Peter will surely be. And Andrew can be counted on to follow loyally, although he is not a leader.

As Jesus looked around the table, He may have known that they did not understand what it was all about. Thomas was always asking questions. Philip had missionary zeal, and some of the others might work out—except Judas.

The future of His mission depended on these twelve. He could not rely on His family, for they had opposed Him at every step and had tried to bring Him home from His mission when He was accused of being crazy. His mother loved Him, but she had sided with His brothers and sisters. And then there was James! Could Jesus have known that James would become the leader of the Church in Jerusalem and stand courageously for his convictions until his martyrdom?

None of them understood. They did not understand His parables, and they had not really understood the acted parable when

He rode into Jerusalem on the ass to symbolize His mission as a suffering Messiah. But perhaps they could see the sacramental meaning of the cross if He could symbolize the significance of His death.

So Jesus, sitting with His twelve close friends, thinking of the coming of God's kingdom and the nearness of His own death, took two simple articles from the table—bread and wine. The meal finished, He blessed the bread with a traditional Jewish prayer. Then He broke it and gave it to them, saying,

"Take; this is my body." (Mark 14:22, RSV)

And then He blessed the cup and they all drank from it, and He said,

"This is my blood of the covenant, which is poured out for many," and He added, "I shall not drink again of the fruit of the vine until that day when I drink it new in the kingdom of God." (Mark 14:24, RSV)

Did they understand? Probably not then. But they never forgot it. In their remembrance of this scene of the Last Supper came their understanding of the significance of the cross and Resurrection.

From our perspective, we can see the significance which the disciples finally saw after the suffering of the cross and the ultimate triumph of the Resurrection. The sacrificial love of Jesus Christ came to its climax in the perfect obedience of the cross, and it is His cross which stands at the center of history. We can sing it:

> "And now, O Father, mindful of the love
> That bought us, once for all, on Calvary's tree,
> And having with us him that pleads above,
> We here present, we here spread forth to thee,
> That only offering perfect in thine eyes,
> The one, true, pure immortal sacrifice." (Hymn 189)

II.

In this supper Christ gives us Himself. A quotation from Augustine applies to us: "I am the food of the full-grown man; become a man, and thou shalt feed on me."[3] "Strong meat belongeth to them that are of full age," says the author of Hebrews (5:14, KJ), who is condemning those who are slow to understand. "For although from the length of your Christian experience you ought to be teaching others, you actually need someone to teach you over again the very elements of Christian truth, and you have come to need milk instead of solid food. For anyone who is limited to milk is unacquainted with Christian teaching, for he is only an infant. But full-grown men have a right to solid food, for their faculties are trained by practice to distinguish right from wrong." (Hebrews 5:12-14, G)

The sacrament of the cross is for mature Christians and not for babes. In Christ's living presence in His Supper, we find fellowship, spiritual sustenance, and love.

From the beginning it has been so. Those men in whom Jesus put His faith at the Last Supper turned out to be pillars of faith. They stood up to persecution, martyrdom, and all kinds of vilification. As far as we can tell, every disciple met a violent death. James, the brother of the Lord, met death in Jerusalem. Paul went through every kind of torture and suffering. Old Polycarp refused to bow down before the Emperor. They had sources of strength which stones, lions, and fire could not overcome. Their resolute courage, their power among men, their persuasiveness and winsomeness, their energy and abundance of life, and their joyous abandon caught the imagination of their converts.

Their source of power came from the living Christ who is pres-

[3] Dorothy Sayers, *Creed or Chaos?* (New York: Harcourt), p. 14.

ent in the life of the worshiping community. His redemptive power is available to you in this sacrament of the Lord's Supper, as you come into Holy Communion with Him. The inward and spiritual grace of this sacrament is yours for the asking.

"I am the food of the full-grown man." From the beginning it was a sacrament of the cross. It is always a sacrament of maturity, for Christianity is strong meat, too strong for babes. It demands the kind of living that is possible only for those who are willing to be tested in fire, who are willing to take up their own cross and follow the Christ wherever He may lead.

> "I know not where the road will lead
> I follow day by day,
> Or where it ends: I only know
> I walk the King's highway." (Hymn 432)

That is enough to know. It is this kind of faith that leads to the peace that passes understanding and to that joy which is glad and adoring. Listen to that great saint of this century, Studdert-Kennedy:

> "Peace does not mean the end of all our striving,
> Joy does not mean the drying of our tears;
> Peace is the power that comes to souls arriving
> Up to the place where God himself appears.
>
> "Joy is the wine that God is ever pouring
> Into the hearts of those who strive with him,
> Light'ning their eyes to vision and adoring,
> Strength'ning their arms to warfare glad and grim.
>
> "Bread of thy Body give me for my fighting,
> Give me to drink thy sacred Blood for wine,
> While there are wrongs that need me for the righting,
> While there is warfare splendid and divine.

"Give me, for light, the sunshine of thy sorrow,
Give me, for shelter, the shadow of thy Cross,
Give me to share the glory of thy morrow,
Gone from my heart the bitterness of loss." [4]

The great sacrament of the cross results in a dynamic and self-giving faith as we come to know "the joy and peace of believing." Within the redemptive community which is the Church, we can be brought to this kind of abundance in living when we meet the crucified and Risen Christ who is really present in the sacrament of His Body and Blood.

---

[4] G. A. Studdert-Kennedy, *The Unutterable Beauty* (London: Hodder & Stoughton), p. 4. Used by permission of the publisher.

10.

THE INEVITABILITY OF THE CROSS

GOOD FRIDAY

PSALM 22:1-19; ISAIAH 52:13-53:12; MARK 15:1-47;

HYMNS 75, 68, 80, 337

"It wouldn't have made any difference to me if Jesus had died of a bad cold." This was said to me by a young theological student. It is a way of putting a question many of us have asked: "What if Jesus had died a natural death?" In other words, does the cross make a difference?

Jesus could have died a natural death if He had wanted it that way. When Jesus was praying at Gethsemane and Judas came with the soldiers, escape would have been easy. It would have been simple to go over the hill and vanish in the darkness. In truth, Jesus did not need to be at Gethsemane at all, for He could have left town and spent the night at Bethany, as He had on the previous nights of that fateful week.

Dr. George Hedley suggests what may have been going through Jesus' mind: "Here was Jesus, with the moonlit city before him, and the deep impenetrable gloom of the olive grove at his back. He had done the best he could, for now almost three years of patient, quiet teaching. What had he achieved? He had gained the hatred of the authorities. He had been alternately hailed and hooted by the crowds. He had been followed only by a few feeble, fumbling peasants. One of them, as he well knew, just the day before had sold him out. The others still were exhibiting petty selfishness over every issue that arose. Three of them, his three best friends among them all, had come with him but now from that upper room and that simple supper; and with the crisis upon them, they had no more imagination than to stretch out and drift off to sleep. What was it all worth?

"Perhaps it was worth trying again, however. Perhaps he could accomplish more if only he could continue his work for a few more years. How easy it would be now, before Judas and the arresting officers came, quietly to disappear among the trees, quickly to scramble up to the summit—and over it, into the wilds where no one could find him, and where indeed no one would bother to follow. He could make his way down to one of the villages near Jericho, go into hiding for a while, ultimately appear again when things had quieted down." [1]

This was a genuine option, just as Socrates had a genuine choice of pardon from his death sentence if he would refrain from teaching.

Jesus' facing of the cross came to a head on this Maundy Thursday evening. That is when He made His decision that the cross was inevitable. He could escape bodily death if He wished, but if He turned and ran it would mean the end of His mission. Not only Jesus' own obedience but the salvation of all the disciples depended upon that decision in Gethsemane.

I.

Jesus must have meditated upon His mission against the background of the Suffering Servant passages in Isaiah. While no Jew had thought of the Messiah as a suffering servant, Jesus saw the connection. The prophet of old was thinking of his nation in exile, and he believed that the Persian King, Cyrus, was the Messiah. But what this unknown prophet of the exile saw, and what Jesus

[1] George Hedley, *The Symbol of the Faith* (New York: Macmillan, 1948), p. 61. Used by permission of the publisher.

so clearly applied to Himself, was the meaning of suffering as a principle of Redemption.

The Church came to see that Jesus fulfilled the prophecy of the Second Isaiah in a way which the prophet could not have foreseen. For we know that

> "upon him was the chastisement that made us whole,
> and with his stripes we are healed." (Isa. 53:5b, RSV)

> "O sacred head, sore wounded,
> Defiled and put to scorn;
> O kingly head, surrounded
> With mocking crown of thorn:
> What sorrow mars thy grandeur?
> Can death thy bloom deflower?
> O countenance whose splendor
> The hosts of heaven adore!" (Hymn 75)

III.

Once the decision in Gethsemane was made, Jesus went through the trial with His head held high. He never faltered, and His opponents were amazed at His spiritual power even when His body failed Him. Yet He was terribly alone; being deserted by all His friends. At His lowest ebb He believed that even God had forsaken Him. And then it was finished. The inevitable cross stands at the center of history.

Jesus could have escaped so easily, and yet He chose to take the consequences of His ministry. To the question, "Was the cross inevitable?" we must answer that it was inevitable at the deepest level of Jesus' nature, although it was not the only possible answer to the coming of the arresting officers. Being Jesus, He would only will one thing, and thus for Him His free choice was inevitably the cross. He made His decision in prayer at Gethsemane, and then

He went alone to die. There was nothing cheap about this death; it was a total self-giving.

Dietrich Bonhoeffer, the German Christian martyr under Himmler, tells us that the cross means that all grace is costly. The trouble with the Church today is that it merchandises cheap grace, sold on the market like a dealer's wares. "Cheap grace," he writes, "is the preaching of forgiveness without requiring repentance, baptism without Church discipline, Communion without confession, absolution without contrition. Cheap grace is grace without discipleship, grace without the Cross, grace without Jesus Christ, living and incarnate." Bonhoeffer tells us we must seek costly grace: "It is costly because it costs a man his life, and it is grace because it gives a man his only true life. It is costly because it condemns sin, and grace because it justifies the sinner. Above all, it is costly because it cost God the life of his Son. . . . Above all, it is grace because God did not reckon his Son too dear a price to pay for our life. . . . Costly grace is the incarnation of God."[2]

So we sing with Abelard:

> "Give us compassion for thee, Lord,
> That, as we share this hour,
> Thy cross may bring us to thy joy
> And resurrection power." (Hymn 68, stanza 4)

IV.

As we meditate upon this inevitable cross in terms of costly grace, we see something of the depth of Christian faith. George Hedley tells the story of a young girl at a revival meeting, who comes down the sawdust trail and kneels briefly at the mourners' bench. Then very quickly rising, she says, "Jesus has saved me." The old evan-

---

[2] Dietrich Bonhoeffer, *The Cost of Discipleship* (New York: Macmillan, 1948), pp. 38-39. Used by permission of the publisher.

gelist pushes her gently back to her knees and says, "No, honey, no! You ain't cried enough yet." [3]

To be a follower of Christ, we have to plumb the depths of suffering. Otherwise we may be the recipients of cheap grace. The cost of discipleship is not cheap. We know that although Jesus wept at Gethsemane, He was almost stoical in his calm attitude afterwards. This does not mean that we have to wait for life to cause us to suffer before we can be disciples, but it does mean that we have to have enough sympathy to understand the suffering of others and especially the suffering of Jesus as He faced the cross. Have you entered fully enough into the mission of Jesus to understand how much He suffered?

But there is another side to the cross which is even more important. Out of the suffering of the cross came victory, which was Jesus' goal. As Bishop Parsons has said, "he sought victory, not death. He found death but he found victory as well." [4] The goal was not the cross but the victory for Jesus' mission that He obtained through the cross. There is a positive note to the cross as we sing:

> "Our sins, not thine, thou bearest, Lord,
> Make us thy sorrow feel,
> Till through our pity and our shame
> Love answers love's appeal." (Hymn 68, stanza 2)

This is a practical fact of life. It is God's way of living out His doctrine in history. Bishop Parsons asks: "Can you save the world by lecturing to it? Can you save it by telling it how the stars work, or what electrons do? Can you save it by building skyscrapers, or making money, or playing baseball? Or even building schools and churches? Some of these things may help it a little, but you never save the world except as men put their lives and their love into it.

---

[3] George Hedley, *The Symbol of the Faith,* p. 64.
[4] Edward Lambe Parsons, *Victory with Christ,* p. 45.

The woman in the school building who, tired and headachy, is drawing the love and stirring the hearts of little children is saving the world. The man who is sitting up nights in that skyscraper, not to make money, but to try to find some way to bring together in a just solution the bitter opponents in an industrial struggle, is saving the world. In all these things it is love, sacrifice, doing for others, making atonement with and for others, that saves the world. And that is what God does in Christ." [5]

"I have been crucified with Christ," says Paul, "nevertheless I live." (Gal. 2:20, KJ) We make Jesus' cross our own, through our imaginations in worship and through our own devoted services in practical everyday affairs.

There is no cheap grace. There is only costly grace. It will cost you much, for the kingdom of God is like that. The kingdom is like a field that holds buried money, like a pearl of great price, so that a man will sell everything to get it. But we still cannot pay the price. It is too much. Jesus Christ died that we may obtain it; and for us now, it demands our total selves.

> "Were the whole realm of nature mine,
> That were an offering far too small;
> Love so amazing, so divine,
> Demands my soul, my life, my all." (Hymn 337, stanza 4)

---

[5] Edward Lambe Parsons, *Victory with Christ* (Cloister), pp. 58-59. Used by permission.

11.

THE MEANING OF THE RESURRECTION

EASTER

COLOSSIANS 3:1-4; JOHN 20:1-10

or PSALM 93; ISAIAH 25:1-9; I CORINTHIANS 15:1-11;

HYMNS 85, 91, 207, 206, 94

The Church is not a memorial society that grieves for its departed Master. The Church has never thought of Jesus as dead. The Church was born because it experienced the living Christ. The Church calls itself "the Body of Christ" because the living Christ is present in our midst. We sing:

"Come, risen Lord, and deign to be our guest;
Nay, let us be thy guests; the feast is thine;
Thyself at thine own board make manifest
In this our Sacrament of Bread and Wine." (Hymn 207)

The central fact of the Christian experience is Resurrection. The Resurrection of Jesus Christ was the basic experience that gave life and direction to the early disciples in the founding of the Church. Jesus Christ was *known* in the primitive Christian community as living in the midst of them. "He was known to have risen because he was known as living."[1]

---

[1] John Knox, *Christ the Lord* (New York: Harper), p. 62.

I.

The earliest list of Resurrection appearances is found in Paul's first letter to the Corinthians:

"For I delivered to you as of first importance what I also received, that Christ died for our sins in accordance with the scriptures, that he was buried, that he was raised on the third day in accordance with the scriptures, and that he appeared to Cephas, then to the twelve. Then he appeared to more than five hundred brethren at one time, most of whom are still alive, though some have fallen asleep. Then he appeared to James, then to all the apostles. Last of all, as to one untimely born, he appeared also to me." (I Cor. 15:3-6, RSV)

Here is to be found the main emphasis of the meaning of the Resurrection. For Christ can be alive in us in the same way as He was alive for Paul. He is a living presence, working out His purpose in and through us.

The other stories point to the same result. The lists of appearances differ greatly in their details, and they cannot easily be reconciled; but whether it be Mary Magdalene, or the other Mary, or doubting Thomas, or the two on the road to Emmaus, the fact is still the same: Jesus is alive! That is the good news of the Resurrection! That is the fact upon which the life of the Church is based!

Professor John Knox tells us that "the knowledge of the resurrection never rested upon such accounts only; it rested upon what was recognized to be the presence of Jesus within the community. It is significant in this connection that although Paul recounts appearances which he has 'received' and expects the Corinthians to be impressed by this evidence, nevertheless he did not himself accept the fact of the resurrection until Jesus appeared to him also. Many to whom such appearances were not vouchsafed were aware of the presence of the Lord Jesus in the fellowship. It was in the experience of that spiritual reality that the faith of the resurrection really consisted."[2]

Even a man who is suspicious of the Resurrection because he knows not the living Christ must accept its significance. Joseph Klausner, the great Jewish scholar, ends his story with Jesus' death. He writes: "Here ends the life of Jesus, and here begins the history of Christianity." For, he says, "the tragedy had an 'epilogue': Christianity would, otherwise, never have been possible."[3] It was no "epilogue," however; it was the climax to the greatest drama ever presented within history. In Paul's letter to the Romans, it is put this way:

"Christ being raised from the dead dieth no more; death hath no more dominion over him. For in that he died, he died unto sin once: but in that he liveth, he liveth unto God. Likewise reckon ye also yourselves to be dead indeed unto sin, but alive unto God through Jesus Christ our Lord." (Rom. 6:9, KJ)

That is the first meaning of Easter: the living Christ is present in our midst because "death has no more hold on him." (G) So we become "alive to God, through union with Jesus Christ." (G)

II.

But Easter has a second meaning. Dr. L. P. Jacks describes Christianity as a "death-conquering religion. . . . Christianity is the most encouraging, most joyous, least repressive, and least forbidding of all the religions of mankind. . . . The end of it is a resurrection and not a burial, a festival and not a funeral, an ascent into the heights and not a lingering in the depths."[4]

"For even as in Adam all die, even so in Christ shall all be made alive." (I Cor. 15:20, KJ)

Out of the Resurrection story comes the hope of immortality,

[2] *Ibid.,* pp. 65-66. Used by permission of Harper.
[3] *Jesus of Nazareth* (New York: Macmillan), pp. 355, 356.
[4] L. P. Jacks, *Lost Radiance,* p. 9.

but the Resurrection in itself does not guarantee our eternal life. We need to remember that only believers saw the Risen Lord. Our future life arises out of this life, for it is because of our faith in the Risen Lord that we have the promise of Resurrection for ourselves. It is something that begins now, and then is carried over into new life.

The same was true for Christ himself. The Resurrection makes sense only against the background of what happened to Him. His previous life, the calling of the disciples, His teaching and fellowship, His passion, the agony of Gethsemane when He accepted God's will that He should die on the cross, and His death are part of the story. We simply cannot understand Easter without knowing the story before Easter. Only those who knew Jesus before Good Friday knew him as the Risen Lord on Easter. Only those in the Church who accept Him with faith can know Him on this Easter.

Christianity accepts death as a fact. "Death," said Augustine, "is an enemy," and it is. "Death," said Paul, "is swallowed up in victory," which is quite different from the sentimental view that death is the final end or that death does not matter because everyone is automatically immortal.

> "The powers of death have done their worst,
> But Christ their legions hath dispersed:
> Let shout of holy joy outburst.
> Alleluia!" (Hymn 91)

But to one who has not experienced the living Christ within the fellowship of the Church, death can be a final defeat.

> "It's all nothing:
> It's all a world where bugs and emperors
> Go singularly back to the same dust." [5]

[5] "Ben Jonson entertains a Man from Stratford," *Collected Poems of Edward Arlington Robinson* (New York: Macmillan, 1929). Used by permission of the publisher.

If Klausner were right, and the closing of the tomb were the final word of authentic Christianity, the world will be given to the worms; but, as Klausner said, "there was an 'epilogue,'" and this turned the whole world upside down. God has accomplished this, "not for anything that we have done but because he chose to do it himself, by the grace which he gave us ages ago in Christ Jesus and has now revealed in the appearance of our Saviour Jesus Christ, who has put down death and brought life and immortality by the gospel." (II Tim. 1:9b-10, M)

In the Burial Office, this same faith is clear when we say, "We commend the soul of our brother departed, and we commit his body to the ground . . . in sure and certain hope of the Resurrection unto eternal life."[6] What is sure is the *hope* of Resurrection unto eternal life, but whether the hope will be fulfilled in relation to a particular person is in the hands of God. So this same prayer may be said over the body of a notorious and evil liver as well as over potential or actual saints.

It is clear that through Christ's Resurrection we are assured of the fact of eternal life as part of existence, and we never exclude anyone from this hope, for God may choose to redeem anyone. But the decision is not made by the minister, which is the reason anyone may be buried with the rites of the Church. What holds in this condition is found in Second Timothy:

"Faithful is the saying:

'If we died with him, we shall also live with him;
'If we patiently endure pain, we shall also share his Kingship;
'If we disown him, he will also disown us;
'And even if our faith fails, he remains true—he cannot prove false to himself.'" (II Tim. 2:11-13, W)

---

[6] Book of Common Prayer, p. 333.

The first letter of John puts it more strongly: "Dear friends, we are God's children now; it has not yet been disclosed what we are to be. We know that if he appears, we shall be like him, for we shall see him as he is. And everyone who possesses this hope in him tries to make himself as pure as he is." (I John 3:2-3, G)

III.

The meaning of the Resurrection is two-fold: First, it arises in the presence of the living Christ in the experience of the disciples. These disciples were first-century Christians who were energized and directed by the living Christ. They took up their crosses and followed Him because He was the Son of the living God, who had suffered and died for their sakes, and was risen again. There are also disciples who are twentieth-century Christians, who also must pay the price of their own crosses if they are to experience the Risen Lord in their midst. It is Christ who is present in our midst now. It is He who answers our prayers, forgives our sins, and gives us grace to do that which He has prepared for us to do. Eternal life begins now in this discipleship. It is now that life begins—not at forty or sixty or death. It is now that we are children of God.

Just as Christ appeared to the women, to Peter, to the twelve, to the five hundred, to James, and finally to Paul, so He appears also to you. We hear Him say, "You, you, why do you persecute Me?" We cry out, "Who are you, Lord?" and He says: "I am Jesus, whom you are persecuting, but rise and enter the city, and you will be told what to do." (Cf. Acts 9:4-6, RSV)

The second meaning of Easter is the portrayal in vivid terms of the identity of persons in the future life. We do not think of disembodied spirits when we know that the disciples by faith could identify the Risen Lord. Resurrection means that there is spiritual identification and that eternal life with God is life in personal terms. We are not absorbed into some spiritual vagueness, but are raised up to the presence of God.

There are no blueprints, and the New Testament is reticent in describing immortality. Furthermore, there is no guarantee, only hope. "We have a sure and certain hope of Resurrection unto eternal life," but we are not told who is to be saved. That is in God's hands. We have the promise that eternal life begins now as we take up our cross to follow Christ. "This is the testimony, that God gave us eternal life, and this life is in his Son. He who has the Son has life; he who has not the Son has not life." (I John 5:11-12, RSV)

As we come to our Easter Communion, we know that

"This the hour of banquet and of song. . . .
Feast after feast thus comes and passes by,
Yet, passing, points to the glad feast above,
Giving us foretaste of the festal joy,
The Lord's eternal feast of bliss and love." (Hymn 206)

12.

DO YOU BELIEVE IN IMMORTALITY?

FIRST SUNDAY AFTER EASTER

PSALM 121; WISDOM 2:23-3:9; REVELATION 1:4-18;

HYMNS 126, 337, 88, 304

We do not think much about immortality during the crisis of the death of a close friend or relative. In the midst of our emotions, we carry through with our old ideas, or we vaguely agree that this person is now safe in the everlasting arms. We are in no position to argue, for if the death has struck close to home we are in a state of emotional shock and cannot think clearly.

But sometimes we wonder if we believe in life after death. We have listened to the great words of the Burial Service, and they have seemed pertinent to the situation, but then we begin to ask, "Do I really believe in immortality?"

I.

Let us look at some of the evidence. We need to admit at the start that there is no proof. We cannot convince anyone who does not want to believe in life after death. Only those who already believe in a loving God are likely to believe in the resurrection of the dead.

Without belief in God, there is no evidence for immortality, for the nature of man does not provide any kind of argument. There is no datum to show that the soul is naturally immortal, as the Greek philosophers taught.

We start not with man, but with God. Because God is good, because God is love, because God is just, because God is our creator, because God is reasonable, we have a basis for our belief.

The first argument for immortality lies in our belief that God conserves whatever is of value to Him. If He has created something that in His eyes is of worth, He will not let such a value disappear from life. It is God who has placed the seal of value on man. To God who loves man, every particular man is potentially valuable.

The evidence for this appears in all religious teachings, and especially in the New Testament. God was sufficiently concerned about man to send Jesus Christ to save us from our sins. God loves us enough to lead us to accept Him as our heavenly Father. The psalmist writes:

"what is man that thou art mindful of him,
  and the son of man that thou dost care for him?
Yet thou hast made him little less than God,
  and dost crown him with glory and honor." (Ps. 8:4-5, RSV)

Throughout Jesus' teachings there is this same emphasis. He treats each individual as if he were of infinite value. Jesus tells us that God loves us as a shepherd cares for his lost sheep. God is overjoyed when we are turned into His fold. And the promise is that we may have eternal life. We are not to have it because we have earned it, for immortality does not depend on what we do. Eternal life is the gift of a loving God. So it is that Job could cry:

"I know that my redeemer liveth, . . . and though this body be destroyed, yet shall I see God: whom I shall see for myself, and mine eyes shall behold, and not as a stranger." (Job 19:25-27, PB)

The Wisdom of Solomon sums it up:

"For God created man for immortality,
And made him the image of his own eternity. . . .

The souls of the upright are in the hand of God
And no torment can reach them." (Wisd. of Sol. 2:23, 3:1, G)

A second argument for immortality stems from the justice of God. It is obvious that many injustices of this life are not corrected before death. The good and devoted people suffer or fail or are defeated, and the evil doers seem to have more than their share of money and power and happiness. Just as Jesus in the Beatitudes promised that the meek and hungry and poor will have a heavenly reward because of their condition, so we believe that God will not let our unjust situations go uncorrected. There is time for God to work out His eternal purpose for each and every one of us.

In the fourth Gospel, Jesus says to His disciples: "Ye now therefore have sorrow: but I will see you again, and your heart shall rejoice, and your joy no man taketh from you." (John 16:22, KJ)

Here is a sure and certain hope of eternal life: that God is just and wills justice for those whom He loves. In the light of this world, there must be a correction of injustice in the world to come.

"There is no place where earth's sorrows
Are more felt than up in heaven;
There is no place where earth's failings
Have such kindly judgment given." (Hymn 304, stanza 2)

A third argument for immortality arises from the second. One of the hardest of all experiences to reconcile with our belief in a God of love is premature death. The death of small children is so poignant that the Church provides a special burial service. The opening sentences include the reminder of Jesus' love for children and this quotation from second Isaiah: "He shall feed his flock like a shepherd: he shall gather the lambs with his arms, and carry them in his bosom." (Isa. 40:11, KJ)

If God is the preserver of what is good, surely He will save for Himself the possibilities of good in a small child. So it seems also with soldiers and sailors and airmen, with young mothers and fathers, and with all who die before they have fulfilled their destiny on earth, God will give them eternal life.

We need to recall that Jesus was in His early thirties when He was crucified.

> "When I survey the wondrous cross
> Where the young Prince of Glory died." (Hymn 337)

The word, young, should be emphasized as it was in the original hymn. Think what would have been lost to the world if Jesus' early death had been the end. The Resurrection is our promise that it is not the end. The impact of Jesus on His disciples came from their conviction that He still lived. They knew that the potentialities hidden in Him were not lost to eternity by His death. A good God will save those who die young.

A fourth argument for immortality lies in the experience of the saints. The best men, the most intelligent scientists and philosophers, the most gifted artists, and the most devoted Christians are people who have accomplished much. In all of them is a conviction that they have been called to a task so large that they can never finish it. All men are called to a task so large that they cannot accomplish it within the finite limits of human history. Even history itself may face annihilation, and still there is God and His purpose. There is so much more to be done, by the great men and by us, that a good God must give us an eternity in which to do it.

II.

Not man but God proves immortality. It is impossible to believe in a good God and not believe in eternal life. This immortality is a gift of God and not man's right. The fourth Gospel puts these words in Jesus' mouth:

"Whoever believes in me, believes not in me, but in him who has sent me. . . . If anyone hears my words, and disregards them, it is not I that judge him, for I have come not to judge the world, but to save the world. . . . I know his orders mean eternal life." (John 12:44, 47, 50, G)

"I am the resurrection and the life, saith the Lord: he that believeth in me, though he were dead, yet shall he live: and whosoever liveth and believeth in me shall never die." (John 11:25, PB)

III.

What, then, is this immortality that we are promised? We have many descriptions—from the Book of Revelation, from the Koran, from the medieval hymns, especially those of Bernard. The streets are paved with gold, but heaven lacks modern plumbing. The following description brings heaven up to date:

"You'll have an eight-cylinder car in heaven—
Air conditioning—
Indirect lighting—
A tile bathroom and a white porcelain kitchen.

"Despite the phenomenal growth of population,
there'll be no traffic problem,
if you would drive out
to the Garden of Eden
for a week end.

"O the celestial sundaes—
all flavors made with the purest chemicals.
No strike—
no speed up—
no lay-off—

everybody a coupon-clipper in heaven,
living in peace, on the eternal drudgery
of the damned.

"All will be fragrant and quiet in heaven,
like the best real estate in Westchester.

"All noise and stench segregated to the underside of the railroad.

"In heaven,
when you want something,
you just fill out an order
and your want is met like magic,
from the Power-Plants
Assembly rooms
Factories
Presses
Forges
Mines
Mills
Smelteries
and Blast-Furnaces
of hell." [1]

That is no worse than Dante's *Inferno* or Milton's *Paradise Lost.* We simply cannot picture what an after-life may be. The Christian religion is remarkably reticent on the subject, but vocal about the fact.

---

[1] Kenneth Burke, "For a Modernist Sermon," *The New Republic,* Dec. 7, 1938, quoted in *The Questing Spirit,* edited by Francis Brentano and Halford Luccock, p. 420. Used by permission.

IV.

Because eternal life is a gift of God, we are not sure who is saved. We know that there is death, even the death of the soul. But if God saves whatever has value, we can judge not, lest we be judged.

Christianity talks of Resurrection rather than immortality, because the essence of the Christian after-life is self-identity. One who is eternally with the Father can say, "I know that I am." Hell is separation from God and eternal damnation is oblivion. Heaven is companionship with God, and eternal life is knowing that we are with God. More than this we cannot say for sure, and thus we rely on poetry and myth and imagery to picture what is not possible for us to conceive in earthly terms.

We do not know accurately what Jesus' Resurrection appearances were. We have many different interpretations of the New Testament stories. But we know that He lives! That does not prove our immortality, but it shows that it has happened.

We do not fear death, then, if God is good. We do not fear death if God preserves what is of value to Him. We do not fear death if God loves us enough to let His only-begotten Son die for us. We do not fear death if great Christians throughout the ages believed that faith in Christ will overcome death. We believe in immortal life as God's gift to us.

> "Jesus lives! thy terrors now
> Can no longer, death, appall us;
> Jesus lives! by this we know
> Thou, O grace, canst not enthrall us . . .
> Jesus lives! henceforth is death
> But the gates of life immortal;
> This shall calm our trembling breath,
> When we pass the gloomy portal." (Hymn 88)

"But as for me, I know that my Vindicator lives. . . .
And I shall see God as my defender,
Whom I shall see on my side,
And my eyes will see to be no stranger." (Job 19:25, 26, 27, G)

"God created man for immortality." (Wisd. of Sol. 2:23, G)

13.

"LORD OF INTERSTELLAR SPACE"

SUNDAY AFTER ASCENSION

PSALM 8; ISAIAH 33:5-6, 17, 20-22; ACTS 1:1-14;

HYMNS 103, 354, 351, 355

After the first Easter, the disciples were aware of the continued presence of the Risen Lord. Not that they had a constant sense of His presence, but from time to time Jesus appeared to them. When these appearances came to an end, shortly thereafter, they had the experience of the coming of the Holy Spirit on Pentecost.

At this Ascension time, we need to recall that the early disciples made their experiences vivid in the only way open to them. They told the story in dramatic and convincing form, using physical expressions to describe what happened to them. How much of their story is to be understood in terms of oriental imagery and how much as actual physical fact we cannot know.

Certainly the Ascension story as recounted in Luke and Acts is based on a spiritual rather than a physical experience. When we say, "He ascended into heaven, And sitteth on the right hand of God the Father Almighty," we are using imaginative and symbolic language. After all, heaven is not up in the sky, and hell is not down in the earth's interior, as some of our ancestors believed before the rise of modern science. No one rides on clouds without an airplane.

The Ascension story offers many difficulties to the literally minded believers. A quite conservative *Commentary* points out that "the outward form of the Ascension was a condescension to human imagination and the ideas of the time."[1] As Christians, we need to understand the message behind the story rather than the particular details of the geography involved.

I.

There are three possible meanings behind the story of the cloud that took the Risen Jesus out of their sight. The first meaning is that Jesus Christ became cosmic. Until the Ascension, the Risen Lord was accessible only to the small band of believers and at the most to about five hundred people. He appeared spasmodically over a period which tradition sets at forty days. But these appearances could not continue indefinitely, and finally they ceased altogether at the time of the Ascension.

The final verse of the Gospel according to Matthew, which has no Ascension story, is relevant here when Jesus says, "Lo, I am with you alway, even unto the end of the world." (28:20, KJ) The Gospel according to John, with no Ascension, ends simply with the fact that the story has been recorded, "so that you may believe that Jesus is the Christ, the Son of God, and through believing you may have life as his followers." (20:31, G) One of the later additions to the Gospel according to Mark says that "the Lord Jesus . . . was taken up into heaven, and sat down at the right hand of God." (16:19, RSV)

Howard Chandler Robbins, in his beautiful hymn for Ascension Day, brings out this meaning:

> "And have the bright immensities
> Received our risen Lord,
> Where light-years frame the Pleiades
> And point Orion's sword?

[1] E. J. Bicknell, edited by Charles Gore, *A New Commentary on Holy Scriptures* (Macmillan), p. 328.

Do flaming suns his footsteps trace
Through corridors sublime,
The Lord of interstellar space
And conqueror of time?" (Hymn 354)

No longer do we think of Jesus within the limitations of nature, manhood, and history, for He is now experienced as active in the total universe. So we speak of the living Christ, the Risen Lord, Who is present with, and in us, in our everyday life. The Ascension is the final escape from the prison of human finitude. Christ is hidden from us, just as He was hidden from the disciples by a cloud, and yet He is with us through the Holy Spirit.[2]

II.

A second meaning is to be found in the phrase, "A cloud received him out of their sight." (Acts 1:9, KJ) The psalmist reminds us that

"Clouds and thick darkness are round about him;
righteousness and justice are the foundations
of his throne." (Ps. 97:2, RSV)

The story of Jesus' transfiguration is centered in a cloud. The disciples were frightened, "and a cloud came and overshadowed them, and from the cloud came a voice,

'This is my Son, my Beloved. Listen to him.'" (Mark 9:7, G)

The story of Israel's escape from Egypt is based on a pillar of cloud by day and a pillar of fire by night.

Christians have never been afraid of the dark clouds with which life overshadows them, because they know that they can always find God in them. When there are clouds of evil, we know that justice

---

[2] See my *Religion Makes Sense* (Greenwich: The Seabury Press), pp. 279-283, for a more detailed treatment of this idea.

and righteousness are backed by the Lord of history. When clouds of life frighten us, there is the promise that if we listen to the message that comes from Jesus there will be a way of overcoming our fears. When we are lost, the darkness will be penetrated by a pillar of fire.

A chaplain, during World War II, recounted his experiences with the heroism and courage of American soldiers. In the tenseness of the dark night before an attack, he was ministering to the wounded and dying, praying with the reconnaissance groups before they began picking at mine fields, riding in an ambulance over a dangerous bridge after a night burial, and throughout all these events there was one recurring theme, expressed as a book's title, *And God Was There*. God was there. In the black clouds of doubt, uncertainty, fear, suffering, and death, God was there.

A certain bishop, after the first year of a happy marriage, lost his wife when their child was born. He came into the chapel the next day, and not seeing the other men praying for him and for her in the chapel, went directly to the altar, and said aloud, "Glory be to the Father, and to the Son, and to the Holy Ghost." Then he turned and walked out.[3] The clouds of life hide God from us, and yet in the clouds we find Him.

"The heaven that hides him from our sight
Knows neither near nor far:
An altar candle sheds its light
As surely as a star;
And where his loving people meet
To share the gift divine,
There stands he with unhurrying feet;
There heavenly splendors shine." (Hymn 354, stanza 2)

---

[3] See W. K. Lowther Clark, *Teaching Sermons* (New York: Macmillan), p. 104.

III.

There is a third meaning to the clouds of Ascension Day. The hymns catch the symbolism of the story:

> "See the Conqueror mounts in triumph . . .
> Riding on the clouds, his chariot,
> To his heavenly palace gate!"

And this is immediately applied to us, for

> "Thou hast raised our human nature
> On the clouds to God's right hand." (Hymn 103)

Just as the clouds received the Risen Lord and carried him to God's right hand, so we may be caught up on the clouds of darkness in our lives and be raised to God's presence.

The heart of the Christian Gospel lies in the transcendence of suffering. We are lifted beyond tragedy, not by escaping it but by going through it. The story of the Ascension goes back through the Resurrection to the cross, and it is Jesus' willing sacrifice on the cross that gives us the clue to all the rest.

Adversity often teaches us more than does prosperity, and in the midst of seeming failure we often grasp hold of those values which give us the proper perspective on life. Shakespeare wrote.

> "Sweet are the uses of adversity;
> Which, like the toad, ugly and venomous,
> Wears yet a precious jewel in his head." [4]

There is power in the Christian religion at exactly this point. Like the boxer who has been knocked down for the count of nine and who, still groggy from that last punch, goes on to win the match, Christians get off the floor of adversity and find themselves given new power by the grace of God to obey His will.

---

[4] *As You Like It,* Act II, Scene 1.

Without these clouds of adversity, men will grow soft. Pleasant, successful living often results in people dull and surfeited by the good things of life. The monotony of life, where all desires are met, needs opposition if people are to come alive again. A simple little poem by Henry Van Dyke says this clearly,

> "If all the skies were sunshine,
> Our faces would be fain
> To feel once more upon them
> The cooling plash of rain.
>
> "If all the world were music,
> Our hearts would often long
> For one sweet strain of silence,
> To break the endless song.
>
> "If life were always merry,
> Our souls would seek relief,
> And rest from weary laughter
> In the quiet arms of grief." [5]

IV.

As we let our imaginations play with the Ascension story, we see the Christ, because He is no longer bound by his humanity, going up to glory as a cloud hides Him from our sight. He has become "the Lord of interstellar space," a cosmic Christ, available anywhere in His universe when "two or three are gathered" in His Name.

For a moment, it must have seemed to the disciples that their Lord had left them for all time, and yet as they looked at the cloud

---

[5] Reprinted from *The Poems of Henry Van Dyke:* copyright 1911 by Charles Scribner's Sons, 1939 by Tertius van Dyke; used by permission of the publishers.

they knew the Lord was there. So, too, as we look at the clouds with which life surrounds us, we know that the living Christ can come through those clouds. He is "the true light, which lighteth every man that cometh into the world." (John 1:9, KJ) "God is light, and in him is no darkness at all." (I John 1:5, KJ) So we can find God in every cloud of suffering, pain, or sin.

And as our imaginations take us one step further, we can see him

> "who makest the clouds thy chariot,
> who ridest on the wings of the wind" (Ps. 104:3, RSV),

and we know that the clouds also can lift us up, for

> "they who wait for the LORD shall renew their strength,
> they shall mount up with wings like eagles,
> they shall run and not be weary,
> they shall walk and not faint." (Is. 40:31, RSV)

As Christ ascended, we pray that "we may also in heart and mind thither ascend, and with him continually dwell . . ."[6]

---

[6] Collect for Ascension Day, Book of Common Prayer, p. 177.

14.

THE SPIRIT'S GOT ME

WHITSUNDAY

PSALM 68; GENESIS 11:1-9; ACTS 2:1-24, 37-42 *or* ACTS 2:1-11;

JOHN 14:15-31a; HYMNS 477, 258, 370, 533

There is an interesting contrast between the stories of Pentecost and the Tower of Babel. Both are dramatic instances of speaking in many tongues. Both involve many people. But Pentecost works for the unity of the people of God, while the Tower of Babel leads to the separation of peoples into many tongues.

The story of Pentecost tells of the experience of people from many countries who heard the disciples speaking, "and they were amazed and wondered, saying, 'Are not all these who are speaking Galileans? And how is it that we hear, each of us in his own native language?' . . . 'We hear them telling in our own tongues the mighty works of God.'" (Acts 2:7-8, 11, RSV)

Peter preached to them, and when they asked him what they should do, Peter said, "Repent, and be baptized every one of you in the name of Jesus Christ for the forgiveness of your sins; and you shall receive the gift of the Holy Spirit.' . . . So those who received his word were baptized, and there were added that day about three thousand souls. And they devoted themselves to the apostles' teaching and fellowship, to the breaking of bread and the prayers." (Acts 2:38, 41-42, RSV)

The story of the Tower of Babel begins at the opposite pole. "Now the whole earth used only one language, with few words."

And men built themselves a city, with a tower that reached almost to heaven. "Then the LORD came down to look at the city and tower which human beings had built. The LORD said,

"'They are just one people, and they all have the same language. If this is what they can do as a beginning, then nothing that they resolve to do will be impossible for them. Come, let us go down and there make such a babble of their language that they will not understand each other's speech.'

"Thus the LORD dispersed them from there all over the earth, so that they had to stop building the city. That was why its name was called Babel, because it was there that the LORD made a babble of the language of the whole earth, and it was from there that the LORD dispersed them all over the earth." (Gen. 11:1, 5-9, G)

All of this is a parable. We know that men did not speak the same language at this point in history, for they evolved from primitive and localized situations throughout the various portions of the globe.

I.

Both stories fit today's world. There was hope of a modern Pentecost when over fifty nations sent their representatives to San Francisco in 1945 and interpreters brought understanding out of many languages. The purpose in the founding of the United Nations was the peace of the world. There was a will to peace at San Francisco that reflected the age-old saying, "Blessed are the peacemakers, for they shall be called sons of God." (Matt. 5:9, RSV)

While the world was rent with strife and while men were dying for a world of peace and freedom, there gathered those who believed in continuing peace and freedom. At least, many representatives gave the appearance of this hope, and they drew the blueprints of a world where there would be food for all, freedom to work, and trust between the nations. This was like Pentecost, for Pentecost stands for the overcoming of the barriers of language, nation, and race.

It was like Pentecost, also, for Pentecost marked the experience of the coming of the Holy Spirit and the Spirit of God entered into the three thousand souls who were baptized. Some of the men at San Francisco were also caught up in the Spirit and they labored mightily for peace. Behind the conference at San Francisco had been previous conferences at Dumbarton Oaks and Bretton Woods, and these findings served as a background for the United Nations charter. The hope of the prophets of old was clearly seen by some as the documents were formulated. Among the Christians, there might have been sung this hymn of hope:

> "In Christ all races meet,
> Their ancient feuds forgetting,
> The whole round world complete,
> From sunrise to its setting:
> When Christ is throned as Lord,
> Men shall forsake their fear,
> To ploughshare beat the sword,
> To pruning-hook the spear." (Hymn 258, stanza 2)

To be sure, there were misgivings. Language barriers could not be completely overcome, for everyone did not mean the same thing by freedom, justice, or democracy. All did not worship the same God, and some did not worship any God, and the delegates could not pray together. The session opened with silent meditation, backed by the prayers of the faithful in Christian, Moslem, Buddhist, and Hindu nations.

There was evidence, even in 1945, of lack of trust, for great nations insisted on their right to a veto power. The Fascist nations were excluded, and some were beginning to suspect the Communist nations.

Notwithstanding the distrust and the greed exhibited by the nations, the Spirit of God was at work in many languages and it seemed for a time that the babble of many voices would be overcome by the will for peace. There was a new chance for mankind, almost a second Pentecost.

III.

One of the reasons behind the story of the Tower of Babel was that God was jealous because their tower was so high. But there was another and more human reason: "Come, let us build ourselves a city, and a tower with its top in the heavens, and let us make a name for ourselves." (Genesis 11:4, RSV)

Before this time when men built their tower to make a name for themselves, they had been able to speak one language, and then it all became a babble. Men also had almost learned to speak one language at San Francisco in 1945, and then came a series of new developments. Hiroshima and Nagasaki changed men's thinking about the power of the atom. What good was Russia's or England's or France's or Nationalist China's power of the veto at a conference table when the United States had the absolute veto of the atom bomb? What good was collective security when the only security lay in nuclear fission?

So the United Nations began to break up into power blocks and spheres of influence before the ink was dry on the signatures of the delegates. Other factors present but disguised at San Francisco came into the open as the Iron Curtain became more formidable than a Maginot Line. The voices of Babel began to take over in market places and political meetings. The firm stand of power politics began to undo the spirit of unity which had almost come into being.

The first Pentecost had led to the formation of the Church, a single Body of Christ which continued Christ's saving work in the world. The Pentecost of the twentieth century had led to the United Nations, a loose federation of autonomous nations in which there was hope of world unity.

The first Pentecost brought men under the Spirit of the living God, and the finger of God pointed to the apostles' teaching and the breaking of bread within the fellowship and the prayers. The Pentecost of the twentieth century held the promise of mutual trust, of feeding the hungry, of faith that men would learn to dwell together in peace in God's world.

But Pentecost never stands alone. Babel voices intruded in the history of the Church; and when the time came, the Spirit led men into diverse channels. Just as God broke men's pride in the story of the Tower of Babel, so God broke the power and pride of a great Church at the time of the reformation. Christendom today is still babbling, and many voices seek to present Christ to the world. And in the divided Church, there is hope in the movement which has led to the World Council of Churches.

If Babel followed Pentecost in the history of the Church, because the Church lost contact with God, so Babel will follow Pentecost again. Unless the Spirit gets hold of men, the forces of evil will conquer.

IV.

Pentecost or Babel? That has always been men's choice. Many voices speak of the saving work of Christ, who died and rose again that we might find the way to repentance through Him and live. Many voices speak in unity in the name of Him who gives life. Many nations resolving to find the way to peace were opened to the Spirit in another Pentecost. Do we listen to the voice of Pentecost? Many states formed a nation over one hundred and fifty years ago, and resolved when they were in danger of drawing apart, that "government by the people, for the people, and of the people shall not perish from the earth." In these words, Abraham Lincoln was a prophet of the Holy Spirit, for only as we believe in "this nation under God" shall we live. The voice of Franklin Delano Roosevelt echoed the same sentiment when he said, "We defend the foundations laid by our fathers . . . We build a life for generations yet unborn. We defend and build a way of life, not for America alone, but for all mankind."

"Thus says the Lord of hosts,

> 'Behold I am going to deliver my people
> From the land of the rising, and the land of the setting sun.
> And I will bring them in, and they shall dwell in the midst
> of Jerusalem.
> And they shall be my people, and I will be their God,
> In faithfulness and righteousness.'" (Zech. 8:8, G)

Or do we listen to the voice of Babel? "War should be the only study of a prince. He should consider peace only as a breathing time, which gives him leisure to contrive, and furnishes ability to execute, military plans." So said Machiavelli. "The very first essential for success is a perpetually constant and regular employment of violence." So said Hitler. Babel comes from this view: "If you wish the sympathy of the broad masses, then you must tell them the crudest and most stupid things."[1] These beliefs of Hitler are matched by fiery crosses and the Ku Klux Klan, by pressure groups and the selfish promotion of class privileges, by racial restrictions and crooked politics, by injustice to the poor and by the denial of civil liberties. "Cure the evils of Democracy by the evils of Fascism!" says Sinclair Lewis. "Funny therapeutics. I've heard of curing syphilis by giving the patient malaria, but I've never heard of their curing malaria by giving the patient syphilis."[2]

---

[1] Adolf Hitler, *Mein Kampf.*

[2] Sinclair Lewis, *It Can't Happen Here.*

The voices of Babel would lead to the paralysis of world trade, to paresis of the world mind, to paranoia of the world peace machinery. And paranoia is a disease which impairs the intellect and leads to homicidal mania because it sees everyone as an enemy.

Karl Marx, perverted as his doctrines were, promised that we should believe in "from each according to his abilities; to each according to his needs."[3] This is an authentic voice of Pentecost when stripped of its materialistic assumptions, and it applies to Russia as well as to the United States. Men have the resources to feed themselves; men have the ability to work out the measures to guarantee peace as outlined at San Francisco; but men are too filled with the spirit of lust and greed and fear to let the Spirit of God speak.

Whenever men are inspired to point to Pentecost as a symbol of the world that can be, they are accused of being dreamers, visionaries, or simply intoxicated. On the first Pentecost, Peter and the apostles were accused of having "had too much new wine" (Acts 2:13, G), and Peter answered:

"'Men of Judea,' he said, 'and all you residents of Jerusalem, let me explain this to you, and pay attention to what I say. These men are not drunk as you suppose, for it is only nine in the morning. But this is what was predicted by the prophet Joel,

> "'"It will come about in the last days, God says,
> That I will pour out my Spirit upon all mankind;
> Your sons and daughters will become prophets,
> Your young men will have visions,
> And your old men will have dreams.
> Even on my slaves, both men and women,
> I will pour out my Spirit in those days,
> And they will become prophets.

---

[3] Karl Marx, *The German Ideology*.

I will show wonders in the sky above,
And signs on the earth below,
Blood and fire and thick smoke.
The sun will turn to darkness,
And the moon to blood,
Before the coming of the great, splendid Day of the Lord.
Then everyone who calls on the name of the Lord will be saved." ' " (Acts 2:14-21, G; Joel 2:28-32)

How many times must our world be bathed in blood before we shall be saved? Can we stand just one more war? Can we return to the Tower of Babel and wait for another Pentecost before the Day of the Lord?

Pentecost means that Christ is with us always. It is a way of saying, "The Spirit's got me." It is another Christmas, as Christ is reborn in us. The Holy Spirit who energized and strengthened and guided Peter and the others on the first Pentecost is also our energizer and strengthener and guide. Pentecost is the only answer to the Babel voices that make our ears dull.

"Yet with the woes of sin and strife
The world has suffered long;
Beneath the heavenly strain have rolled
Two thousand years of wrong;
And man, at war with man, hears not
The tidings which they bring;
O hush the noise, ye men of strife,
And hear the angels sing!

Above its sad and lowly plains
They bend on hovering wing,
And ever o'er its Babel-sounds
The blessed angels sing." (Hymn 19, stanzas 3 and 2)

On this Whitsunday, we need to hear the song of the angels. We need to overcome the voices of Babel with the voice of Pentecost. We need to pray

> "Spirit divine, attend our prayers;
> Make a lost world thy home;
> Descend with all thy gracious powers;
> O come, great Spirit, come!" (Hymn 370, stanza 5)

15.

THE TRINITY AND FREEDOM

TRINITY SUNDAY

PSALM 29; ISAIAH 6:1-8; EPHESIANS 4:1-16;

HYMNS 266, 145 (TUNE 479-1), 267, 274

Belief in the Trinity guarantees our freedom. Because we believe in God the Father, God the Son, and God the Holy Ghost, we are no longer slaves to custom or to the state or to our own inner sense of inadequacy.

Dr. A. V. G. Allen, the great historian, wrote that there is a greater emphasis on belief in the Trinity in the Episcopal Church than in the other communions of Christendom, and that this is a reproduction of the ancient charter of genuine freedom. "In almost every part of the Prayer Book it appears; it is the constant, ever-recurring refrain, it opens the service, it is appended to every psalm and canticle, it is the essence of the creeds, the formula of blessing. It would not have been made so prominent if it were not closely connected with that which is most dear to every human heart, freedom from the shackles without, freedom from fear in the inner life of the soul, freedom from every tyranny whether of Church or State. For the doctrine brings freedom by the proclamation of the co-equality of the Son with the Father, since Christ is therefore placed above kings and thrones must henceforth retain their power by obedience to the will of Christ. . . . The doctrine of the Trinity is the Magna Charta of religious liberty."[1]

---

[1] A. V. G. Allen, *Freedom in the Church* (New York: Macmillan, 1907), pp. 3-4. Used by permission of the publisher.

I.

Let us look at some implications of this statement in terms of social pressures, political restrictions, and our own inner insecurity.

All of us are not so timid as Casper Milquetoast, but often we are like the guest at the White House who came down to breakfast and was filled with confusion as he observed the president calmly pouring a portion of his coffee in a saucer and dousing it with sugar and cream. The guest immediately did the same, and then saw the president place the saucer on the floor for the cat.

We do not like to be conspicuous by our awkwardness, by our failure to be at ease, or by appearing to be different in dress or mannerism. Many of us simply do not dare to be ourselves, to stand for the hard right against the easy wrong, to witness to our Christian faith in a world of pagans. We feel constrained by the pressures from without. We are shackled by the customs and manners surrounding us.

We see this among our children, who are sensitive to their differences from other children at school. They want the same kind of clothes, the same types of amusement, the same customs among their parents. They will do anything to conform to their peers. This is perfectly normal at the pre-adolescent or adolescent stage, and parents should be sympathetic and helpful.

Adults show these same childish traits in their refusal to talk about political or religious matters. We are too shy to witness to Christ or to Christian standards in public places, or even to invite a friend to attend Church with us. Some of us go to the extreme of trying to show that we are a regular fellow by using the obscene language of some of our friends, by drinking too much with others, or by letting little dishonesties pass without even a disapproving glance.

We have become so used to living in a society where pagan

standards are accepted that we calmly agree with our acquaintances who do not go to Church. "Yes, I know," we say, "Church is a luxury for you." Or we say, "Yes, I go to Church, but I'm a regular person just the same."

Such slaves to custom and social pressure are not really free.

II.

Our freedom is also restricted by the State. While our democratic ways protect us from the totalitarian pressures of European nations, we still allow many special interest groups to lobby for legislation that is against the good of the majority of the people. In some areas, we have restricted the civil liberties of minority groups or of special occupations. Certain kinds of taxation have hidden limitations for our pocketbooks that we refuse to recognize.

What freedom we have was obtained by fighting for it, and then by writing it into the law of the land. But we have allowed infringements on that freedom, including limitations placed on one group for the benefit of another. Even freedom of speech is jeopardized.

We should remember the story of the two soldiers who were fishing. A Swiss guard on one side of the river was reeling in the fish, while the Nazi guard on the other side was catching nothing.

"Why is it," the German called out, "that you are having such good luck? Are we not already using the same bait yet?"

"Yes," said the Swiss, "but on this side the fish are not afraid to open their mouths."

The Church believes in political and religious freedom, and it needs to take a stand against the current infringements on liberty.

III.

Our freedom is restricted by social pressures and political action, but behind these is the basic cause of our inability to be free. James Norman Hall in his poem on *Fear* writes:

"The thing that numbs the heart is this:
That men cannot devise
Some scheme of life to banish fear
That lurks in most men's eyes."[2]

Men cannot devise a scheme, because fear is not overcome by men or by human schemes. When we bow to social pressures or to political intrigue, it is fear of the conspicuousness or consequences that keeps us from standing upright. We are afraid of what our friends will think, of the opinion of the boss, of our own inner aches and pains.

Worry, anxiety, and fear, grounded often in unreality, operate to keep us from being our true selves. Worry, anxiety, and fear, when based on facts, cannot be overcome by refusing to face the real conditions.

This inward fear, this lack of spiritual security, this fundamental anxiety, is the basis for our loss of freedom in other realms. It is at this point that the doctrine of the Trinity is relevant.

IV.

In Paul's second letter to the Corinthians, he talks of the Lord as Spirit. Then he says, "Where the Spirit of the Lord is, there is liberty." (3:17, KJ) "There the heart is free." (B) "There is open freedom." (M)

Nicodemus could not understand the conditions of freedom. "How can a man be born when he is old?" he asked. (John 3:4) And this is the answer, "That which is born of the Spirit is spirit. Do not marvel that I said to you, 'You must be born anew.' The wind blows where it wills, and you hear the sound of it, but you do not know whence it comes or whither it goes; so it is with every one who is born of the Spirit." (John 3:6-8, RSV) And we also re-

---

[2] James Norman Hall, *Fear* from *Pocket Book of Quotations,* p. 91.

ceive this message: "You will understand the truth, and the truth will set you free." (John 8:32, M)

This answer carries us into the center of Christian belief. Our belief in the Trinity lets us see God as the one who made us, Christ as the one who came that we might be saved through Him, and the Holy Spirit as the source of power to make us obedient servants of the Holy Trinity. If Christ is our King, then no earthly ruler, no social pressure, no political action, and no inward fears can take away our true freedom in Him who is our King.

"What then shall I fear?"

"For freedom Christ has set us free; stand fast therefore, and do not submit again to a yoke of slavery. . . . For you were called to freedom, brethren; only do not use your freedom as an opportunity for the flesh, but through love be servants of one another. . . . For in Christ Jesus [nothing] is of any avail, but faith working through love. . . . But now we are discharged from the law . . . so that we serve not under the old written code but in the new life of the Spirit. . . . For all who are led by the Spirit of God are sons of God." (Gal. 5:1, 13, 6; Rom. 7:6, 8:14, RSV)

This freedom based on faith in the triune God is not a freedom in isolation or in the next world. It is freedom operating fearlessly in the present world, with the hope of perfect freedom in the world to come. The freedom that is based on the Lordship of Christ says that governments must bow down before Him, that customs must be in the spirit of holiness, that a brave new world must come which will express the ideals of the kingdom of God.

The Christian knows that there can be no genuine freedom for the few while there is only freedom to die from starvation or from want of work or from political assassinations and purges for the many. Abraham Lincoln saw this clearly when he said,

"Our reliance is in the love of liberty which God has planted in us. Our defense is in the spirit which prizes liberty as the heritage of all men in all lands everywhere. Destroy this spirit, and we have planted the seeds of despotism at our own doors. Those who deny freedom to others deserve it not for themselves, and, under a just God, cannot long retain it. This country, with its institutions, belongs to the people who inhabit it. Whenever they shall grow weary of the existing government, they can exercise their constitutional right of amending it; or their revolutionary right to dismember and overthrow it. Why should there not be a patient confidence in the ultimate justice of the people? Is there any better or equal hope in the world?" [3]

William Pierson Merrill catches this same spirit in his great hymn.

> "Not for battleship and fortress,
> Not for conquests of the sword,
> But for conquests of the spirit
> Give we thanks to thee, O Lord;
> For the heritage of freedom,
> For the home, the church, the school,
> For the open door to manhood
> In a land the people rule." (Hymn 145, stanza 2)

"The doctrine of the Trinity," said A. V. G. Allen, "is the Magna Charta of religious liberty." It is more than that; it is the basis of all personal and political liberty as well; for only a people nurtured by faith in God the Father, who is the ruler of all creation, and in God the Son who is our redeemer, and in God the Spirit who acts through us to strengthen and guide us—only such a people can rule with liberty and justice for all.

---

[3] Quoted by Wade Crawford Barclay, *Challenge and Power,* p. 160.

16.

"STIR-UP" SUNDAY

SUNDAY NEXT BEFORE ADVENT

PSALM 145; JEREMIAH 3:14-18; JAMES 1:12-27; HYMNS 524, 519, 536, 535

As we come to the end of the Church year, our symphony of the seasons builds to a climax. The collect for this Sunday reads:

"Stir up, we beseech thee, O Lord, the wills of thy faithful people; that they, plenteously bringing forth the fruit of good works, may by thee be plenteously rewarded; through Jesus Christ our Lord."[1]

The evidence does not point toward an affirmative answer to this prayer. Many people say today that the Church has fallen into innocuous desuetude, which means simply harmless disuse. For these people, religion is classed with the horse and buggy, with Edison's first phonograph, or even with the medieval period of feudalism when the Church was dominant in political affairs. Christians are all right in their place, and so is a museum. Some of us, even when we go to church, are like a certain Eutychus, who fell asleep while Paul was preaching, "and being overcome by sleep, he fell down from the third story and was taken up for dead. But Paul went down and bent over him, and embracing him, said, 'Do not be alarmed, for his life is in him.' And when Paul had gone up and had broken bread and eaten, he conversed with them a long while, until daybreak, and so departed. And they took the lad away alive, and were not a little comforted." (Acts 20:9-12, RSV) The church is a place of safety, as long as people do not sit in windows

[1] Book of Common Prayer, p. 225.

during the sermon. If this is all that it stands for, why bother to get up from a comfortable bed?

If the Church is in such a serious condition, certainly its members will be jarred awake if the estimate of this century made by Professor Einstein is true. Writing for the Time Capsule prepared for the New York World's Fair in 1939, to be opened in A.D. 6939, he said:

"Our time is rich in inventive minds, the inventions of which could facilitate our lives considerably. We cross seas, relieve humanity from all muscular work, and have learned to fly and utilize electric waves to send messages. . . . However, production and distribution of commodities is entirely disorganized, so that everybody must live in fear of being eliminated from the economic cycle. Furthermore, people living in different countries kill each other at irregular intervals, so that anyone who thinks about the future must live in fear." [2]

Anyone who thinks about the future must certainly live in fear, yet religion is fallen into a state of innocuous desuetude. I wonder what correlation there is between these two statements. People are full of fear and frustration, and yet religion is harmless and impotent.

Einstein suggests that the difficulty lies in the fact that "the intelligence and character of the masses are incomparably lower than the intelligence and character of the few who produce something valuable for the community." [3] What an inadequate statement this is! It was the few who obtained power in Germany and drove Mr. Einstein and Thomas Mann and Karl Barth and Paul Tillich and many other gifted people out of Germany. And I don't see the scientist, among the intellectual few, doing anything to save the world, not even Mr. Einstein, fine as he is.

---

[2] *Reader's Digest,* December 1938, p. 77.
[3] *Loc. cit.*

I.

The fears that Einstein listed are genuine fears, magnified many times over since 1939. But his few who produce something valuable for the community have not overcome men's fears. Indeed, Mr. Einstein's work in the field of atomic fission has done much to add to our fears. The genius who improves our mechanical gadgets and other scientific inventions does not provide an answer for men's insecurity. The tools which scientists create may be used to rebuild or to destroy civilization, and at this moment in history the odds are on the side of destruction.

When Jesus taught men to overcome fear, to practice brotherhood, and to enter the kingdom of God, he did *not* say, "Behold the day will come when scientists will invent television so you can listen to sermons and see the choir singing from your easy chair. Verily I say unto you, the time will come when you can fly to heaven and meet your maker in a Super DC-6. When you have cleared the slums, then you will no longer have the poor with you. When your enemy strikes you, be sure to have the biggest guns and the fastest planes and the hydrogen bomb on your side." He said simply, "Repent, for the kingdom of God is at hand."

The Jews saw the same thing, and when Malachi talked of the future it was in terms of God's messenger:

> "For he shall be like a refiner's fire,
> And like fuller's soap,
> And he shall sit down as a refiner and a cleanser of silver,
> And shall cleanse the sons of Levi." (Mal. 3:2b, 3, G)

II.

Even with the words of the prophets ringing in their ears, there are those who believe the Church to be harmless, and even boring.

Christopher Morley, making a pun on the great words *Te Deum,* has written a bit of rhyme called "Tedium Laudamus."

> "Even in the church, where tedium is prolific,
> I hail thee first, Episcopalian bore:—
> Who else can serve as social soporific
> And, without snoring, teach the rest to snore?"[4]

Eutychus is not the only one who has fallen asleep, and it has not always been the listener's fault. But no one went to sleep when Jesus was preaching to the five thousand. Indeed, they were so wrapped up in what He was saying that they forgot their hunger for food because of their hunger for His teaching. No matter how badly the Church has been prostituted by those who put people to sleep, the purpose of the Christian faith is to stir them up. The letter of James put this sharply:

"Obey the message; do not merely listen to it and deceive yourselves. For anyone who merely listens to the message without obeying it is like a man who looks in a mirror at the face nature gave him, and then goes off and forgets what he looked like." (1:22-24, G)

There is no need to join Eutychus or to apply the term innocuous desuetude to the Christian faith. Religious faith has power to stir people deeply and profoundly. William James recounts the experience of a Swiss hiker who was overcome by a tremendous experience while on a hiking trip:

"I was in perfect health: we were on our sixth day of tramping, and in good training. . . . I felt neither fatigue, hunger, nor thirst, and my state of mind was equally healthy. I had had good news from home; I was subject to no anxiety, and there was not a shadow of uncertainty about the road we should follow. I can best describe

---

[4] "On a Certain Cleric," *Bartlett's Quotations* (11th ed., Boston: Little), p. 213. Used by permission of the author.

the condition in which I was by calling it a state of equilibrium. When all at once I experienced a feeling of being raised above myself, I felt the presence of God—I tell of the thing just as I was conscious of it—as if his goodness and his power were penetrating me altogether. The throb of emotion was so violent that I could barely tell the boys to pass on and not wait for me. I then sat down on a stone, unable to stand any longer, and my eyes overflowed with tears. I thanked God that in the course of my life he had taught me to know him, that he sustained my life and took pity both on the insignificant creature and on the sinner that I was. I begged him ardently that my life might be consecrated to the doing of his will. I felt his reply, which was that I should do his will from day to day, in humility and poverty, leaving him, the Almighty God, to be judge of whether I should some time be called to bear witness more conspicuously. Then, slowly, the ecstasy left my heart; that is, I felt that God had withdrawn the communion which he had granted, and I was able to walk on, but very slowly, so strongly was I still possessed by the interior emotion. . . . The state of ecstasy may have lasted four or five minutes, although it seemed at the time to last much longer."[5]

God catches some men in ecstasy and stirs them up so that they always desire to do His will. Other men He reaches through the channels of prayer, of listening to His message and obeying it. And still others God finds through the operation of the human conscience as it becomes more and more sensitive to the good and evil motives of men. In these and many other ways, God stirs up the wills of his faithful people, and their good works make it clear that religious faith is dynamic and positive in its impact on men and society.

As long as our hearts are filled with despair, mistrust, doubt, and

---

[5] *Varieties of Religious Experience* (New York: Longmans, Green, 1902), pp. 67-68. Used by permission of the publisher.

suspense of moral judgment, defeat is certain—both in our own lives and in the achievement of justice among men. But when men are stirred up to seek victory through faith, the results are significant. The achievements of men through faith, as they are supported by the grace of God, are indicated in our faith in the great ideals of the human spirit, faith in one another, faith in human and social justice, faith in the fundamental decency of the human race even when we know men are sinners, faith in the power of God to change men so that they can exercise their faith. "We are justified by faith," says Paul. This faith is an attitude of mind, an intention which results in real ethical decisions pointing in the direction of God's will.

III.

Christian faith can fall into innocuous desuetude only when men allow it to happen. When men fall asleep in the presence of God, fear enters their hearts. There was a man who, because of a slight injury to his brain, suffered from a form of sleeping sickness. No cure seemed possible and he was kept in bed. One day, when the nurse was not looking, he fell out of bed onto his head, and the jar of the fall broke the hold of his sickness and he returned to normal life. He had been stirred up by a jarring experience. Religion reaches some people the same way. Only a jarring experience can awaken them to the responsibilities of Christian living.

The Latin word which we translate "stir up" is *excita*. This also means arouse or set in motion, to encourage or stimulate. It is our job, yours and mine, to be stirred up and aroused by the will of God, that we may in turn arouse and encourage the Church to set in motion the good works that are needed in this day. Jesus said: "The harvest is plentiful, but the laborers are few; pray therefore the Lord of the harvest to send out laborers into his harvest." (Luke 10:2, RSV)

Professor Einstein saw correctly the value of inventive minds who have provided so many accessories for comfortable living, but "the intelligence and character of the few who produce something valuable for the community" are not the necessary tools for solving the problem of the basic sickness of our culture. Furthermore, as long as the Churches suffer from a form of sleeping sickness, their efforts will result in innocuous desuetude. Some Church members are like the fearful servant who buried his talent, because he did not dare to put it to proper use. Others make excuses when the Lord calls them, just as they did in Jesus' stories, but Jesus did not accept their excuses. He knew that they didn't care enough, and that their desires to bury their dead and get married were ways of refusing to put first things first.

A tremendous challenge is held out to us. We sing

> "Rise up, O men of God!
> The Church for you doth wait:
> Her strength unequal to her task;
> Rise up, and make her great!" (Hymn 535, stanza 3)

The Church year ends with Stir-up Sunday. This exciting note is the finale of the symphony of the Christian year, where faith expresses itself in action.

"Now what use is it, my brothers, for a man to say he 'has faith' if his actions do not correspond with it? . . . To the man who thinks that faith by itself is enough I feel inclined to say, 'So you believe that there is one God? That's fine. So do all the devils in hell, and shudder in terror!' For, my dear short-sighted man, can't you see far enough to realise that faith without the right actions is dead and useless? . . . Yes, faith without action is as dead as a body without a soul." (James 2:14, 19-20, 26, P)

"Stir up, we beseech thee, O Lord, the wills of thy faithful people; that they, plenteously bringing forth the fruit of good works, may by thee be plenteously rewarded; through Jesus Christ our Lord. *Amen.*" (PB, p. 225)

Part Two

17.

THE WORK OF THE LAITY

MEN'S ADVENT CORPORATE COMMUNION
OR *LAYMEN'S SUNDAY*

PSALM 138; ISAIAH 62:1-12; III JOHN 1-15;

HYMNS 576, 575, 572, 574

At a small church in Asia Minor, some time around the turn of the first century, there were two leaders who portrayed opposing approaches to the Church's work. There was Diotrephes, who was conceited and who loved to be head of everything, but who refused to welcome the brothers and even excommunicated them. There was also Demetrius, who had the warm recommendation of the elder in Ephesus.

"I have written briefly to the church," wrote the elder, "but Diotrephes who likes to be their leader will not accept what I say. So if I come, I will bring up the things which he is doing, and how he is maliciously accusing me. Not content with that, he refuses to welcome the brothers himself, and he is interfering with those who want to do so, and has them put out of the church. . . . Everyone testifies to Demetrius; the truth itself does; I testify to him, too, and you know that my testimony to him is true." (III John, 9-10, 12, G)

We are not sure of the characters in this reference. The elder may have been a presbyter or bishop, and it is certain that he was a man of authority. Whether Diotrephes or Demetrius were ordained, we do not know. But it would not be far-fetched to apply this text to our laity.

I.

The Episcopal Church has inherited a developing responsibility which is placed on lay people. Before the Reformation, the Church was pretty much in the hands of bishops. The laity had a hand in the Reformation and in the approval of the Book of Common Prayer. The doctrine of the priesthood of all believers meant that the laity were no longer second-class Christians.

This belief was expanded in the Church in America. Bishop William White believed that the laity should have a hand in the government of the Church and in the election of bishops and rectors. He quoted Richard Hooker's view that only the "general consent of all" gives form and vigor to the laws of the Church.

The authority of the Church in America rests primarily in the General Convention, and all new legislation and formulation of doctrine as well as changes in the Prayer Book and Hymnal, must be approved by the laymen and clergy in the House of Deputies as well as by the House of Bishops.

The development of the parish as the basic unit of the Church's life freed the people from too strict episcopal control. The responsibility of laymen on the vestry included not only responsibility for the material welfare of the parish but also for the selecting and calling of a rector. From the parish, men and women serve and legislate in the diocese as well as in the synod and General Convention.

Throughout the Church, lay people have important responsibilities. Strong movements for work among both men and women now permeate the life of the Church from the smallest mission to the staff of the National Council of the Church.

II.

In contrast with this ideal view of the place of the laity, there are some facts which are disturbing. In most levels of responsibility, the laity let the clergy take the lead. To a certain extent this is inevitable (as a consequence of the training and competency of the clergy and in deference to their professional status) but when the laity withdraw from the basic responsibilities of being a Christian with the attitude of let the clergy do it, the work of the Church is seriously and sometimes fatally handicapped. There are about seven thousand clergy and over two million lay people. It is only by a proper use of the two million that the Church's work will be done.

The challenge held out to those who are not fulfilling their vocations as lay members of the Church is found in this wonderful hymn:

"Come, labor on.
The enemy is watching night and day,
To sow the tares, to snatch the seed away;
While we in sleep our duty have forgot,
He slumbered not." (Hymn 576, stanza 2)

III.

The most significant work of the laity lies in evangelism. An evangel is simply one who carries good news; he is a messenger of the Gospel. "To evangelize is to confront men with Jesus Christ, so that they will put their trust in God through him, and by the power of the Holy Spirit live as Christ's disciples in the fellowship of the Church."[1] When Jesus selected seventy of his followers, all of whom were lay people as distinct from the twelve disciples who

---

[1] Randolph C. Miller, *The Clue to Christian Education* (New York: Scribner), p. 8.

had a special mission, he sent them out to proclaim the good news.

When anyone publishes the glad tidings by his life, his influence, his speaking, or his work in the Church, he is an evangelist. In fact, every Christian is either a good or bad evangelist. Some of us hide the information that we are Christians, and when it is discovered, our influence is negative because it has made no difference in our lives. Some of us are obnoxious Christians and, while we talk loudly about our Church affiliation, we disprove the value of Christian faith by our pride. Some of us are properly modest, because we know that our Christian faith is not backed up by knowledge of the true nature of the Church, and we need help in finding out how to witness to the power of Christ and to assist in making the local parish be truly a Christian congregation.

This latter stage provides the proper condition for doing something about our personal faith and our parish life. A recent development in adult Christian education proceeds along these lines and meets these needs. Several small groups from neighboring parishes come together for a long week end, beginning Friday with dinner and concluding some time Sunday afternoon. They are provided with expert leadership for their discussions, but no speeches are permitted by anyone. Normally, such a conference begins with the question, "What does your parish do?" It does not take long for a blackboard to be covered with the many details of parish life. Perhaps there is some bragging about the size of the Church school, or the amount of money raised by the Woman's Auxiliary, or the number of excellent choirs for all age groups, or the fine family-style parish suppers, or the interracial nature of the congregation. Many of these achievements are quite notable and deserving of praise.

Then comes a second question, "How Christian are these activities? Could they exist unchanged in a school or social group or community concert?" This leads the lay people to ask a fundamental question: "What is the purpose of Christianity?" and sooner or later the discussion turns to the problem of redemption. Here are all these wonderful parish activities, but to what extent can any parish activity provide for salvation? Who was reborn at the last sewing circle? Who found the wings of faith at the last parish supper? Who felt the power of the Gospel at the meeting of the young people? Did the word of God reach the congregation during a recent sermon?

These are extremely uncomfortable questions, and the groups usually find themselves depressed as they are forced to answer that in their parishes the processes of redemption are not at work in an effective way. A Church school teacher asks what to do when a boy upsets her lesson plan, and the counter-question is asked: "Are you more concerned with the redemption of the lesson plan or in the salvation of Johnny?" Another teacher wants to know why the boys and girls in the tenth grade have been quitting Church school, and another teacher tells how he keeps his group of the same age together by bringing the good news to them in terms they can hear. Then comes the question, "Can people hear the Gospel in the King James version or in the language of the Prayer Book?"

Questions such as these can go on for hours, and at most conferences the whole of Saturday is spent on them. Each parish group begins to see its own congregation in new terms. All these activities are worth nothing unless the power of Christ to redeem men is mediated through them. They begin to see the meaning of the great drama of Redemption as revealed in the Bible,[2] and how it applies on the local level. They begin to evaluate their own parishes in new terms, for unless the parish is a redemptive and redeeming fellowship it is not fulfilling its responsibility as an evangelical power for Christ.

Out of the depression and despair of analysis comes the hope of

---

[2] See sermon for second Sunday in Advent, "Education for Redemption," p. 12.

Christian faith. There is a "gospel gladness" (a grand phrase) which is to be proclaimed. The purpose and work of the laity become clearer when they see their responsibility as evangelists in these terms, for they go back to their parishes with the tools as well as the insights for leading their congregation from darkness into light.

"Come, labor on.
Claim the high calling angels cannot share—
To young and old the gospel gladness bear:
Redeem the time; its hours too swiftly fly.
The night draws nigh." (Hymn 576, stanza 4)

In one way or another, this redemptive group works together to increase the efficiency of the parish for Christian ends. They can say with Paul:

"I appeal to you therefore, brethren, by the mercies of God, to present your bodies as a living sacrifice, holy and acceptable to God, which is your spiritual worship. Do not be conformed to this world but be transformed by the renewal of your mind, that you may prove what is the will of God, what is good and acceptable and perfect." (Rom. 12:1-2, RSV)

IV.

The Church is not vague about putting such responsibilities on the laity. In the Offices of Instruction it is quite clear:

"My bounden duty is to follow Christ, to worship God every Sunday in his Church; and to work and pray and give for the spread of his kingdom."

This is a summary of the evangelical duty of every lay person, regardless of age, sex, or color. When we are confirmed and accept Jesus Christ as Lord and Saviour, we are saying, "I will worship God every Sunday in Church, and not just when I feel like it, not out in the woods but in Church." There it is. There is no exception to the rule, except obvious Christian responsibilities or illness.

This is the beginning of our evangelism. Our witness to our own faith in Christ is our attendance at worship. Participation in the fellowship of common worship provides our strength to bring others into the redemptive fellowship. The dynamic worship of the congregation of faithful people, where the word of God is preached and the sacraments are duly administered, becomes the source of redemptive power in every other parish activity, so that we use every parish outlet to "work and pray and give for the spread of his kingdom." The word of God, however powerfully it may be preached, never makes an empty pew leap for joy. But there is joy in heaven over one sinner who repents.

The kinds of work each individual may do to fulfil his responsibility as an evangelist will vary with his abilities and opportunities, but the call is clear:

> "Come, labor on.
> No time for rest, till glows the western sky,
> Till the long shadows o'er our pathway lie,
> And a glad sound comes with the setting sun,
> 'Servants, well done.'" (Hymn 576, stanza 5)

The task of the laity is a high one. It involves the government of the Church with all the details of administration, the formulation of doctrine, and the revision of the Prayer Book and the hymnal, the development of canon law and the acceptance of men for the ministry. But chiefly, the task of the laity is an evangelistic one, whereby they work and pray and give for the spread of the kingdom.

As we work through the various organizations of the parish, as we take part in an Every Member Canvass, as we perform those jobs in and around the church which are essential to the ongoing life of the Church, we need to remember what the Church ought to be: a redemptive and redeeming fellowship, a channel whereby God's forgiving and strengthening grace comes to each and every member, an outgoing and outreaching group which seeks to draw men to the "gospel gladness."

As lay evangelists, we need to remember Diotrephes, who thought he could lord it over the brethren, for each of us is likely to relish the power that comes from responsibility. We need to remember that the elder intended to bring up all the malicious sayings of Diotrephes. The example of the lay evangelist is Demetrius, for "everyone testifies to" him, "the truth itself does."

"Let your light so shine before men, that they may see your good works, and glorify your Father which is in heaven." (Matt. 5:16, KJ)

18.

A RACE REBELLIOUS

THEOLOGICAL EDUCATION SUNDAY[1]

PSALM 132; ISAIAH 30:1-21; I TIMOTHY 5:17-25;

HYMNS 255, 220, 218, 219

The people of Israel were being offered faith in the power of Egypt as the solution to their dangers. The strong arm of a friendly neighbor was the best guarantee for keeping the peace. This position was challenged by the prophet Isaiah, who held a position of authority. Isaiah claimed that this reliance on Egypt was a false security based on illusions, and that only a quiet faith in God could provide the necessary strength. He wrote:

> "It is a race rebellious
>   a faithless brood,
> children who will not listen
>   to any of the Eternal's laws,
> who refuse visions from their seers,
>   and true words from their prophets,
> who would have only smooth things told them,
>   only illusions prophesied." (Isa. 30:9-10, M)

This text speaks clearly to our age, for we have been a rebellious race, putting our faith in military force and in power politics. A Gospel that promises us salvation has been turned down by the

---

[1] Sunday nearest St. Paul's Day.

vote of the majority. Even in our churches there have been "smooth things told" us and we have heard "illusions prophesied."

If ever a world needed guidance, it is this world of ours. When the framework of our thinking includes world-wide wars, saturation bombing, and political maneuvering on the basis of expediency, we need more than "the blind leading the blind." (Luke 6:39) When our outlook on life is indicated by a fundamental insecurity and when mental illness is on the increase, we need a process of integration of our personalities which is not offered by the culture in which we live.

With all the glories of a mechanical age and with all the meanings of freedom in a democracy and with all the insights of a highly civilized culture, we are not finding the resources for a mature faith. We do not know what it means when Isaiah says,

> "By returning and resting shall you be saved,
> In quietness and confidence shall be your strength."
> (Isaiah 30:15, G)
> "Your strength is quiet faith." (M)

I.

The message of God for any generation is proclaimed by the Church. The message of the Church lies with the ministry. The clergyman is parson, pastor, priest, and preacher. He brings the good news of the redemption of the world in Jesus Christ to the people of his generation. He leads the people in their quest for a redemptive and redeeming fellowship in which every member has access to the grace of God through faith.

The word parson means simply the person who is outstanding in the community. In previous times, the parson was frequently the best educated man in town and today he is still the expert in religious knowledge. He is qualified to provide authoritative testimony in all fields where religion bears on life.

The pastor is the shepherd who cares for his flock. He leads them, watches after them in sickness and in health, and counsels with them as they seek a way out of the confusion and turmoil of life. He brings to bear, on their problems, the wisdom and the power that come from God.

The priest is set apart for specific functions, including the celebrating of Holy Communion and giving assurance of God's pardon and blessing. He is a representative of the people in their worship of Almighty God.

The preacher is called to give the people the word of God. He is not simply an expert giving his own religious ideas; he is a man under authority, and it is his task to interpret the revelation of God in Jesus Christ to his people. He is a prophet whose lips God makes eloquent "for righteousness that shall all evil break." He brings not only the good news of hope but also the judgment of God's justice.

II.

Where does our clergyman come from? How is he called?

Every minister was first a layman. This is the only source of the ministry. He is a man who in some way has received a call from God to the priesthood of the Church. He has a sense of vocation. Just as Jesus called the fishermen from their nets to be the first disciples, so the hand of the living Christ reaches out today and draws men into His service in the ministry of the Church.

But this call may only seem genuine, and the Church has set up physical, mental, and spiritual safeguards. A man must pass physical and psychiatric examinations and be approved by his rector, vestry, bishop, and standing committee before he is recommended for study in the divinity school, where there are further checks on his capacity to serve the Church. There are texts for this: "It seemed good to the Holy Ghost, and to us." (Acts 15:28, KJ) "Never be in a hurry to ordain a presbyter." (I Tim. 5:22, M) "Never ordain anyone hastily." (G) "As for the imposition of hands, do not bestow it inconsiderately. . . . Some men have faults that are plain to view, so that they invite question; with others, discovery follows upon the heels of enquiry; so it is, too, with their merits; some are plain to view, and where they are not, they cannot long remain hidden." (I Tim. 5:22, 24-25, K)

III.

When a man whose call is approved by the Church has obtained his college degree, he goes to one of our theological schools or seminaries. Here he learns to be parson, pastor, priest, and preacher.

As a parson, he learns about the Bible: how and when it was written, to whom the various portions were addressed, what each book says, and what it means as a record of the mighty acts of God. He is taught how the Church came to be, how it expanded into alien cultures, how it was broken into bits by necessary reformations, how it stands today at the outposts of the world after a century of the greatest missionary expansion in its history. He becomes an expert in the knowledge of Christian truth as it is found in the Bible, in history, and in men's minds today.

As a pastor, he learns about people. He is trained to be a practical helper, to lead them into a deeper devotional life, to teach them to pray, to assist them in their troubles, to counsel with them in their problems. He receives training in social welfare agencies, jails, hospitals, and rural areas. He knows the principles of mental hygiene and when to call in a doctor or psychiatrist. He takes courses on counseling. He learns about the Christian education of children and adults within the framework of the Church as a redemptive and redeeming fellowship. He develops a knowledge of right and wrong based upon the teachings of Christ. He receives all the tools he needs to make practical the love of people, which comes to him as a gift from God.

As a priest, he learns about public worship. He is taught the history of the Church at prayer. He knows the contents of the Book of Common Prayer, to which he promises to be loyal. He is taught how to conduct all sorts of services to meet the needs of the people under any conditions. He becomes "a strong intercessor for pardon, charity, and peace."

As a preacher, he is taught both how and what to preach. All that he learns in the divinity school is relevant to life, for it is when the Gospel speaks to men and men hear it, that God acts to redeem men from their sins. The preacher will convict us of sin, he will offer us the good news of the Gospel of Jesus Christ, and he will bring us the resources of the Church which is the fellowship of faithful people. Whether he will be a prophet cannot be determined by the seminary, for only as God touches his lips will prophecy come from his mouth, but he will be awake to human needs, condemning our pagan ways, and showing us the judgment of God upon the sinful ways of our culture. Out of this combination there will always be the promise of salvation through faith in Jesus Christ our Lord.

There is nothing of the ivory tower about this kind of ministerial education. There is much that the clergyman must learn that is highly specialized and technical, but it is always based upon the relevance of the Gospel to the fundamental needs of men. The Episcopal Church is turning out men who are better trained for the exacting work of the ministry today than ever before in its history.

In the seminaries you will find devoted and capable men and women on the faculties. They are leaders of the Church. They write books for all to read, including the well-known THE CHURCH'S

TEACHING series. Most of them have had extensive experience as parish priests, so that they see the connection between what they are teaching and the demands of the ministry. They combine profound scholarship (matching that of any denomination) with practical insights leading to effective service in the Church. Many of them are teaching at a financial sacrifice, for the average seminary does not have enough money to match the salaries of the larger parishes in which they might otherwise be serving.

IV.

Our concern is to understand the relation of the laity to our seminaries. One theological school has a board of trustees made up entirely of laymen. Boards of trustees of most divinity schools are made up equally of bishops, priests, and laymen. These groups establish the basic policies, make the financial decisions, award the degrees, and approve the personnel of the faculty and administrative staff.

A second concern of lay people for the theological schools is that the source of supply of students is among laymen exclusively. The recruiting of students is a lay operation. The quality of a seminary's graduates depends upon the kind of students applying for admission. When our lay people take seriously the need for a ministry of the highest calibre, it will mean that they will actively participate in the encouragement of the right young men for the ministry.

A third concern is the financial support of the theological schools. The Presiding Bishop has designated Theological Education Sunday as the opportunity for every parish and mission to hear about theological education and to support it financially. There are twelve seminaries spread about the country, from the Episcopal Theological School in Cambridge, Massachusetts, to the Church Divinity School of the Pacific in Berkeley, California. Most of these schools are overcrowded with students, and at the same time they do not have the financial resources to meet the new demands of increased student bodies. Most of them have little income from endowment; the tuition charges are nominal, and they rely, for their running expenses and capital expansions, on the annual gifts of interested lay people. There are capital gifts for the endowment of professorships and construction of buildings or parts of buildings; there are annual pledges over a period of years to underwrite the budget; and there is the annual offering on Theological Sunday. As congregations throughout the land give with understanding and generosity, the increased giving will make our seminaries more effective.

A fourth concern is the interest and prayers of the people. If you live near a seminary or pass near one on a trip, plan to make a visit and see for yourself. If a member of your congregation is at a divinity school, remember him in your prayers and write to him occasionally. Your parish will certainly want to underwrite a portion or all of his expenses. As you come to know the seminaries, include them in your prayers.

V.

The ministers of tomorrow are not going to preach "smooth things" or "prophesy illusions." They will be too well-educated in the truth of God for that. They are going to plant mustard seeds of faith which will grow into overpowering convictions. They are going to plant and water, and God will provide the increase. The care of all the churches will be upon them, as they were upon Paul. They will be valiant, as they seek to make firm foundations on faith in Jesus Christ for the coming of the kingdom of God.

I am convinced that the hope of the Church, and thus the hope of the world, lies in the kind of leadership we provide in the Church. The secret of our success is the theological school, in which we provide training of a calibre as high as that found in any professional school. Just as we need money for cancer research and for polio and for the other physical ills of mankind, so we need money for spiritual research. We need money for libraries, for superior faculty members, and for adequate equipment. A ministry of reconciliation, whereby Christ is the redeeming power in our parishes and missions, is the goal of all training for the ministry. Nothing can be more important than this.

I am content to teach in a seminary for the rest of my days, for there is no other calling so important as the preparation of men to be parsons, pastors, priests, and preachers. God is saying, "This is the way; walk in it." (Isa. 30:21, G)

19.

DO WE LOVE ONE ANOTHER?

RACE RELATIONS SUNDAY

OR *QUINQUAGESIMA*

PSALM 119:33-48; DEUTERONOMY 10:12-15, 17:11-1; I JOHN 4:1-21;

HYMNS 536, 263, 262, 493

> He who claims enlightenment, and all the while hates his brother, is in darkness still. (I John 2:9, K)

The Miami Clipper lands in New York, and a Christian from Puerto Rico seeks out the nearest church the following Sunday and is told he is not wanted. A Chinese Christian lands in San Francisco to attend the University of California and has difficulty finding lodging in Berkeley.

A few years ago, a group of Irish Catholics in Boston were terrorizing the Jews, chiefly by beatings, and it took a New York paper to publicize it. The Boston papers did not dare to publish it until the news came from New York.

In a crowded trolley car in New York City, a Negro who was evidently under the influence of drugs made a scene with his shouting and raving. It caused some of the white people to say to themselves, "Negroes are like that." When he got off the car, two middle-aged Negroes with fine, serious faces were standing in the aisle, and one said bitterly, "That's why we can never get anywhere." They knew that no one on the trolley would remember the respectable Negroes, but that some unthinking whites would assume that the drugged Negro was typical.[1]

The Oriental suffers in the same way: Americans of Japanese ancestry were unceremoniously herded with other Japanese into concentration camps during the war.

Some casual visitors to New York City report, "The trouble with New York City is that there are too many foreigners there: Jews, Negroes, Slavs, Puerto Ricans, and so on." Yet all of them are Americans. New York City was originally Dutch; Florida and California were originally Spanish; New Orleans was French; much of Pennsylvania was German; Negroes arrived in America with the earliest settlers. The earliest American, the Indian, having been separated from American culture by the system of reservations, has probably received the rawest deal of all.

I.

There is hope that conditions will improve. There is evidence that they are improving. When interracial relations were about to receive a setback in the Church, and the faculty of a seminary resigned in protest over the refusal to consider applications from Negro students, the trustees reversed their position. At the same time, the Church made plans for a nonsegregated General Convention in the south. Our only Negro bishop is in Liberia, but when the Bishop of Washington was consecrated, one of the attending presbyters was a Negro and one of the co-consecrators was Chinese.

The Christian teaching is clear: "If any one says, 'I love God,' and hates his brother, he is a liar; for he who does not love his brother whom he has seen, cannot love God whom he has not seen.

---

[1] William Scarlett (ed.), *Christianity Takes a Stand* (New York: Penguin), p. 78.

And this commandment we have from him, that he who loves God should love his brother also." (I John 4:20-21, RSV)

Charles Lamb tried to get around this injunction by saying, "Don't introduce me to that man! I want to go on hating him, and I can't hate a man whom I know."

A Christian, says Paul, is "a new self newly made in the likeness of its creator." (G) "In this new man of God's design there is no distinction between Greek and Hebrew, Jew or Gentile, foreigner or savage, slave or free man. Christ is all that matters, for Christ lives in them all." (Col. 3:10-11, P)

This is very easy to say, but the causes of racial prejudice are so deeply ingrained that an intellectual approach will not suffice. Furthermore, the caste lines of our society are reflected in the Churches, so that the Churches are often more segregated in fact than are the schools, restaurants, and hotels. Much of our thinking is the unconscious acceptance of distinctions growing out of past cultural patterns.

Buell Gallagher summarizes such thinking as follows:

> "Any white man is 'better' than any non-white, therefore
> All contacts between whites and non-whites must in some manner express this differential; and thus
> The etiquette of caste must always be observed; and consequently
> The white man's floor is the Negro's ceiling." [2]

Not only is there unconscious acceptance of this kind of thinking, but the basic pattern of life in America is based upon it. A child born into American society does not have the option of deciding whether he will have a casteless society. He grows up in the

---

[2] Randolph Crump Miller (ed.), *Church and Organized Movements* (New York: Harper), p. 98.

midst of color caste. He can accept it, consciously or unconsciously. He can modify it as he becomes conscious of its evils. But if he reacts violently against the system, he is likely to be an outcast himself. Except among certain minority groups, he is sure to walk alone if he rebels. Not even the Church will back him up.

In order to provide balance for this difficult situation, we need to recount the experience Relman Morin describes in an Associated Press dispatch during the Italian campaign of World War II. "A German prisoner was brought past the encampment one day; he gaped with surprise when he saw their faces and asked if they were Japanese. An interpreter explained that they were Americans of Japanese parentage. The German shook his head in wonder and said: 'Ach! that's American!' "

Also on the positive side is the number of actual friendships that exist across the boundaries of racial difference. People who really know members of minority or persecuted groups rarely hate them. People who know Negroes as friends and fellow-workers are less likely to be prejudiced than those who know them only as wage earners or servants. There is less friction in nonsegregated neighborhoods, where the races are completely intermixed, than in areas where there are dividing lines. Missionaries who have spent many years with the people of a different race find they have no prejudice at all.

Social patterns move slowly, but there has been enough opportunity in America for some people from the racial minorities to become outstanding citizens. It is obvious when we think of George Washington Carver, the scientist, Daniel Hale Williams, the surgeon, Walter White of the National Association for the Advancement of Colored People, Jackie Robinson of the Brooklyn Dodgers, Dorothy Maynor as she sang at the inauguration of President Eisenhower, and Ralph J. Bunche of the United Nations. It is obvious when we think of Albert Einstein, who is a German-Jewish refugee, or Fritz Kreisler the violinist, or Henry Morgenthau who was in President Roosevelt's cabinet, or Bernard Baruch.

William Gorgas, who conquered yellow fever, was a Dutch Protestant; Knute Rockne, the great football coach, was a Norwegian Roman Catholic; Igor Sikorsky, the airplane engineer, is Russian Orthodox; Andrew Carnegie was a Scotch Protestant; Arturo Toscanini is an Italian Catholic. Look at the names on the football roster of the Fighting Irish of Notre Dame or of any professional baseball club.

Between the races there have been amazing incidents of fellowship and cooperation. A group of Jews offered to work for nothing on Christmas so Christians could be at home or church. Everyone remembers the four chaplains—Protestant, Catholic, and Jewish—who went down with their ship after giving their life belts to others. A store owned by a white man in Harlem was protected by Negroes during a Negro riot.

II.

On this question, the Christian position is obvious. We find it summarized in John Oxenham's hymn:

> "In Christ there is no East or West,
> In him no South or North,
> But one great fellowship of love
> Throughout the whole wide earth.
>
> . . . .
>
> Join hands, then, brothers of the faith,
> Whate'er your race may be!
> Who serves my Father as a son
> Is surely kin to me." (Hymn 263, stanzas 1 and 3)

Individual Christians have achieved this ideal, often at great sacrifice to their personal position in society. They have been willing to give up their lives in the fight against prejudice and bigotry, in order to find their lives in the service of their fellowmen. They have been ministers of Christ in the work of reconciliation.

The Churches as a whole, however, have failed tragically to face the problem. The Methodists gave way to segregation by setting up a central jurisdiction for Negroes, although Negroes are not barred from membership in individual congregations. Other denominations have been so dominated by whites that Negro membership is negligible, even in segregated congregations. While the largest Episcopal congregation in the country is in Harlem, the Episcopal Church has failed to provide enough Negro ministers even for the few congregations that need them.

Again there are elements of hope. The Episcopal Church refused to accept an invitation to have its General Convention in Houston until it was assured that there would be no segregation. The Churches bring pressure on hotels and restaurants whenever they select a city for a convention, although the sharp answer of one hotel manager was a judgment on the Churches. He said, "I will open the doors of my hotel to Negroes when the Churches of this city do the same."

The Churches as a whole have backed civil rights legislation, although the National Council of the Churches of Christ has been less outspoken than the previous Federal Council of Churches because of a wider base of representation.

This sermon does not pretend to have an answer to the problem, but on this Race Relations Sunday we need to face it. No matter where we stand as individuals or as Churches on this question, we stand under the judgment of the Father of Jesus Christ who created all men to be free and equal. We know that in Christ there are no distinctions of race or class. Not only the ideal but the command of the Gospel is that all shall be treated equally as human beings. We stand under the judgment of the Gospel. "He who claims enlightenment, and all the while hates his brother, is in darkness still." (I John 2:9, K)

We cannot be content to stand under judgment, for "the burden is intolerable." We stand under a command, which is to

"Turn back, O man, forswear thy foolish ways." (Hymn 536)

Each of us must make his own decision in the light of the command of the Gospel. The sin, the injustice, the discrimination, and the fallacy are present. If we are against sin, we are against discrimination.

We may prefer a gradualist approach, moving slowly toward the goal of eliminating color caste, being satisfied with one step at a time. We need to start where we are, and in different areas of a community we are on various levels. We need to use education, legal procedures, and persuasion.

Whatever we succeed in doing, we stand under God's judgment. If we do nothing, then God's judgment is without hope, for the day of the Lord is darkness and not light to those who disobey Him. If we seek to reform the Church, we need to remember the prayer of the Oriental: "Revive thy Church, O Lord, beginning with me." As we are cleansed from the sin of prejudice, we will be in a position to channel some of God's redemptive power into the congregation, and as the Church is strengthened it will cooperate with other forces seeking to provide equal opportunity and "liberty and justice for all."

"Till all the distant people
In every foreign place
Shall understand his kingdom
And come into his grace." (Hymn 262, stanza 3b)

20.

CHRISTIAN PARENTS

MOTHER'S DAY

OR *CHRISTIAN FAMILY SUNDAY*

PSALM 78:1-12; PROVERBS 31:10-31; LUKE 2:40-52;

HYMNS 504, 214, 514, 296

> Without Joseph and his mother knowing it, the boy Jesus stayed behind in Jerusalem. . . . And when Joseph and Mary saw him, they could hardly believe their eyes, and his mother said to him,
>
> 'Why have you treated us like this, my son? Here have your father and I been very worried, looking for you everywhere!' . . . Then he went home with them to Nazareth and obeyed them. (Luke 2:43, 48, 51, P)

We usually treat this story from Jesus' point of view to show how brilliant he was as a quiz kid. We rarely look at the parents' angle.

To begin with, Mary and Joseph were active members of their religion. His parents, we are told, "went to Jerusalem every year at the feast of the Passover." Good Jews were expected to do this, but it took time and money. It indicated that the pilgrims were keeping the law and were doing what the priests expected. The religious practices in the home were very likely the orthodox Jewish requirements; and Jesus in His home life must have learned much from the lore of His inherited religion. His parents did not send Him to Jerusalem; they went themselves and took Him with them.

A twelve-year-old boy usually exercises a good deal of freedom. He goes and comes very much in terms of his own independence. Jesus seems to have been no exception. There must have been a large crowd of pilgrims leaving Jerusalem along the road to Nazareth, and Joseph and Mary did not check whether their boy was in the crowd until nightfall. This indicates that they treated Jesus in a typical way, without too much overprotectiveness. When they found him missing, however, they promptly retraced their steps with great anxiety. After a day's search (for they had walked one day each way to make a total of three days), they finally located Jesus. He had obviously expected that they would know where to find Him, and he showed no concern over having been left behind. He was in the most natural place in the world and was seeking the most natural knowledge from the experts. (Note that Jesus was "listening and asking questions," not teaching His elders.)

The parents did not understand their twelve-year-old boy, and the reply confused them: "But why did you look for me? Did you not know that I must be in my Father's House?" (P) He went home with them, and the reader is relieved to know that He was obedient. "And as Jesus grew up in body and mind, he grew also in the love of God and of those who knew him." (P)

Jesus' position in this situation is made clear if we remember that at the age of twelve, Jewish boys were admitted to the status of "Son of the Law." This made them responsible for the discharge of their religious duties. Jesus had been trained by Joseph and by the local rabbi to understand religious teachings and duties. So He took seriously His new status by remaining in the temple where He could further His education. Any boy loves to question the experts, and Jesus' natural curiosity was aroused by this unparalleled opportunity.

I.

This beautiful boyhood scene from the life of Jesus provides much information for modern parents. Christian parents today are not much different from Jewish parents in the first decade of the first century. Neither are adolescent boys and girls much different from what we see of Jesus in this story, except that His sense of vocation was established at an earlier age. From what we know of Jewish family life in those days, we are sure that Joseph and Mary were to a great extent responsible for His earliest religious convictions.

As we look at the responsibilities of Christian parents today, we find the same concerns. Just as Jesus was exposed to the Jewish rituals of His day, so are children today baptized and confirmed. When a child is baptized, more is begun than is at the time effected. God acts directly on the child, but He also acts on the child through persons. Whatever God does through the act of pouring water, we know that He acts also through the parents, godparents, and congregation to provide adequate nurture of the child.

This role of Christian parents in Baptism has not been sufficiently appreciated in modern times, due primarily to a misunderstanding of how much the Church can accomplish through its Sunday schools. The teaching function of the Church is performed by parents just as much as by teachers and clergymen.

We know that the child depends on his parents for his birth and survival, both physical and spiritual. The relationships of a child with his parents dictate the development of his personality before there is contact with the external environment. To the young preschool child, it may well be said that the parents are the Church! The priesthood of all believers is expressed as parents teach their infants and young children.

When the parents are Christian believers, they teach partly by their words, but chiefly through what is called the language of relationships. A child knows that God is dependable because his parents are dependable; and his parents are dependable because they, in turn, depend upon God. Thus, the Church acts through the home. Of course, this ideal is not often achieved, but is it not the goal of Christian parenthood?

Let us see how home relationships illustrate the Christian Gospel. A child needs acceptance, love, discipline, freedom to grow, and the sense of outreach toward mystery. When he is accepted for what he is, it means that the child is part of the fellowship of the family, with recognition of his differences, peculiarities, and sex. The love that is offered him by his parents is a complete self-giving, a willingness to love when the child is most unlovely, for it is when the child is most demonic that he needs love most desperately. Christian parents can provide this because the power of God is in them to help overcome their natural hates and frustrations and egoisms. Both acceptance and love operate within the framework of discipline, for only through law and order do we provide consistency and simplicity. A play-pen is not primarily to keep the child in, but to keep the world out! A fence is a law surrounding freedom. The sense of discipline is rooted and grounded in the justice of God's absolute sovereignty. As the child grows, he continues to need acceptance, love, and discipline, but these must expand in order that he may be stimulated to grow. Always beyond him and beyond his parents, there is the outreach toward the mystery of God and His universe, so that the possibilities of development are unlimited. These relationships can exist in every home for every member, no matter how young or old he may be.

Have you ever thought what is involved psychologically when a child slaps his mother? It is his encounter with freedom to reject authority. He unconsciously wills his mother's death, although it is she upon whom his own existence depends. Thus, he alienates himself from the source of his existence and wills his own damnation.

There is here a momentary desolation, which he cannot overcome by his own power. When the child slaps, swears at, or in other symbols rejects his mother, he is separated from the creative source of his own life. Nothing he can do can re-establish his relationship with her. He cannot win back her love by anything that he does, not by reform, not by offering a gift or bribe, not by providing a scapegoat or alibi, not even by self-punishment. There is only one way in which the love relationship can be established; the parent comes to life by offering her love to the separated child. Only the parent can bridge the gap—through healing-love. This is an experience often repeated. The parent may punish the child to indicate the reliability of justice, but redemption can come only as the parent pays the price.[1]

It can be seen that the cross stands at the center of parental love, as it stands at the center of God's suffering love. For men also sought to kill God, they alienated themselves unalterably from God's presence by turning their backs on Him, by their sin, and by the most grievous sin of killing God's unique Son. Yet the Father by His love was willing to restore men to the relationship of sonship when they turned to Him in faith.

This pattern of death and resurrection as found in the center of Christian faith is repeated throughout life. The new birth of Baptism follows the death of the self; the one who loses his life shall save it; the Prodigal Son was dead and is alive again. "In the same way," says Paul, "look upon yourselves as dead to the appeal and power of sin but alive and sensitive to the call of God through Jesus Christ our Lord." (Rom. 6:11, P)

II.

Parents as teachers provide a series of relationships which are fundamentally religious. They provide a climate of opinion that

[1] See *The Clue to Christian Education* by Randolph C. Miller, pp. 64-65.

makes Christianity a center of daily living expressed in the experiences of the home. They give, by their example and their atmosphere, the answers to the fundamental questions of children.

The child, as young as three or four, is in some way or the other asking these questions:

"Who am I?"
"Who are you?"
"How did we get here?"
"Where are we going?"

Are not these the basic questions that you and I are asking? The child learns the answers to these questions by the language of relationships in the home. The child is what he is treated as in the home. Is he wanted, loved, treated with the dignity due a child? Is he part of the fellowship of the home? And are the parents agents of God's love, devoted to Christ and His Church, just and durable, with sufficient empathy to look out on the world through the eyes of a child? Are we the products of God's love? Or did we come from nothing, and is this home going to hell or oblivion? Is life made up of pale pastels of surface meanings? Is this a secular world or God's earthly community?

If parents have such responsibilities as this, surely they need the Church. They need the Church's guidance, but they need much more than guidance. They need the Church's fellowship, for only as they are part of God's family in a regular and responsible way will they be able to incorporate the things we have been talking about into their lives. Above all, they need the Church's worship, for the Church is a channel of God's grace, and grace is the power to approximate God's will. Only by this means can parents come into their deepest relationship with God, where God will mend the brokenness of their own lives and give them His healing love to bind them together in harmony.

III.

We have seen, then, that home and Church may be likened to Siamese twins. If you cut the blood stream between them, both may die. Neither can exist properly without the other. The family and congregation are inseparably bound together to be God's agents in the care and nurture of children.

The parents of Jesus knew this. They made their home a haven of peace, and they instilled in their son the sense of the majesty of God. Jesus was able to believe that God was like a father because He lived in a home where fatherhood and motherhood had meaning for Him. As He reached adolescence, He expressed His independence and His sense of mature responsibility by seeking out the wisest leaders of Judaism in order to gain greater wisdom. So He grew in wisdom and in stature, and in favor with God and man, including, we may believe, with His parents, to whom He was obedient until the call came at the time of His baptism to go forth on a greater and more dangerous and more glorious business.

Christian parents today have no more difficult task than Jewish parents in the first century. It is the task that it has always been, but perhaps we see it more clearly. For we have the redemptive act of God in Christ as a pattern, and we know that God was in Christ reconciling the world to Himself.

There is a priesthood of parenthood, which is the child's protection against all the pressures of a secular world. It gives him the rhythm of death and resurrection, of rejection and acceptance, of judgment and mercy, of sin and forgiving love, that will follow him all the days of his life. Because he knows the security of the love of Christian parents, he will grow into the assurance of the love of God.[2]

---

[2] Cf. Reuel L. Howe, *Man's Need and God's Action* (Greenwich: Seabury, 1953), for a fuller treatment of this theme.

"O Christ, thyself a child
Within an earthly home,
With heart still undefiled,
Thou didst to manhood come;
Our children bless, in every place,
That they may all behold thy face,
And knowing thee may grow in grace." (Hymn 504, stanza 2)

21.

"AS A FATHER PITIETH HIS CHILDREN"

FATHER'S DAY

PSALMS 103; PROVERBS 3:1-12, 4:1-12; MATTHEW 6:7-14;

HYMNS 504, 308, 505, 533

> Yea, like as a father pitieth his own children; even so is the Lord merciful unto them that feai him. (Ps. 103:13, PB)
>
> As a father is kind to his children, so the Lord is kind to those who revere him. (G)

One of the most daring and awesome concepts given to men is the belief that God is like a Father! Think what it must have meant in the days when men thought that deities were fearful heavenly beings, completely unpredictable and capricious, powerful without responsibility, nonmoral and capable of receiving a bribe. Against this conception there came, with shattering force, a new idea: "like as a father pitieth . . . so is the Lord merciful unto them who fear him."

To those who had known no pity, who felt no mercy in the hands of an angry deity, here was epoch-making news! God *is* capable of pity, and pity means sympathy, compassion, commiseration. To be able to feel the sufferings of His children was the most important characteristic of God, who is like a Father.

This same insight of the psalmist is translated as kindness. Early concepts of deity knew nothing of kindness, for no primitive god was capable of forgiveness. Even in the Bible, we find that Yahweh was not often benign or tender or lenient or friendly. Yet, when it was seen that God is kind, these attributes were attributed to Him. God is merciful. So today we sing John Milton's paraphrase of Psalm 136:

> "Let us, with a gladsome mind,
> Praise the Lord, for he is kind:
> For his mercies aye endure,
> Ever faithful, ever sure." (Hymn 308)

I.

The idea of God's Fatherhood was derived directly from human fatherhood. Today, the process is reversed. We discover what human fatherhood ought to be because we know what Jesus tells us about divine Fatherhood.

It is not hard to be a father in the simplest sense, for a father is simply a begetter, a male parent. But such fathers are not necessarily thought of with love and adoration on Father's Day. It is the Christian concept of divine Fatherhood, derived from what we know of the Christian God, that gives meaning to Father's Day. A human father, like God, is a creator. He has power for good or evil. He is idolized by his children. He determines how his children shall grow up, within the limitations of human freedom.

Part of a father's gift to his children is heredity. He cannot do much about it, except to thank his ancestors and those of his wife, but the fact remains that a child resembles his father in terms of both character and physical appearance. It is said "nearly every man is a firm believer in heredity until his son makes a fool of himself."

While a father can do little about heredity, he can do much about environment. An old saying about Diogenes is that when a man's son swore, Diogenes struck the father! Today we talk more about delinquent parents than about delinquent children.

It is hard for a father to accept his children's badness, especially when he knows deep down in his heart that his children are actually copying his bad habits. A child imitates his father's posture, vocabulary, attitudes, prejudices, and moral values. Even when there is friction between father and child, the child will often acquire the father's habits which the child hates.

If a child is to learn the meaning of the Fatherhood of God, he will gain this knowledge through his experience of his own father. This has led some Christian educators and psychologists to conclude that it is better not to teach the Fatherhood of God at all, because many children reject the concept. Dr. C. H. Valentine, an English psychologist, observes: "It is often found that in the patient's childhood his father stood as the representative of authority, punishment, superiority and power. The very name 'father' stands to some patients as the symbol of a 'power-psychology.' For that reason, the idea of God is either repudiated or accepted with terror. The fatherhood of God does not mean to them the way of forgiveness, love and fellowship, but the way of discipline, severity and guilt."[1] Rather than reject the idea of fatherhood, Dr. Basil Yeaxlee concludes "that parents possess a power far greater than they know, and . . . it can be . . . exercised . . . to produce results more splendid and enduring than they imagine."[2]

There comes a time, however, when the father finds his authority challenged. The days of uncritical, childlike devotion vanish, and suddenly the father is challenged by all the vagaries of adolescence. The fifteen-year-old wants freedom, and a new form of relationship must replace the old one. This same thing must have happened once to God, when men first exercised their freedom and ceased

---

[1] *Treatment of Moral and Emotional Difficulties,* p. 140, quoted by Basil Yeaxlee, *Religion and the Growing Mind* (Greenwich: The Seabury Press), p. 56.

[2] Yeaxlee, *Religion and the Growing Mind,* p. 187.

to be followers of instinct only. It is likely that mankind is still in its adolescence in relation to our heavenly Father.

II.

In a letter written by an old man in Ephesus about the year A.D. 100, there are these remarkable words:

"Dear children, I am writing to you,
because your sins are forgiven for his sake:
fathers, I am writing to you,
because you know him who is from the very beginning:
young men, I am writing to you,
because you have conquered the evil One.
Children, I have written to you,
because you know the Father:
fathers, I have written to you,
because you know him who is from the very beginning:
young men, I have written to you,
because you are strong, and the word of God remains within you,
and you have conquered the evil One." (I John 2:12-14, M)

"Now this is what he commands, that we believe in the name of his Son Jesus Christ, and love one another as he has commanded us to do; he who obeys his commands remains within him—and God remains within him. . . . If our heart does not condemn us, beloved, then we have confidence in approaching God, and we get from him whatever we ask." (I John 3:23-24a, 21, M)

When Jesus presents this same idea, he draws the analogy from human fathers:

"Well, if for all your evil you know to give your children what is good,
how much will your Father in heaven give good to those who ask him?" (Matt. 7:11, M)

Men came to believe that God is as good as human fathers, and this was a great advance over more primitive ideas of God. Now, in Jesus' teaching, human fatherhood simply does not compare with God's love for men. "God shows his love for us in that, while we were yet sinners, Christ died for us." (Rom. 5:8, RSV) God's love is sacrificial love, a love that gives all for His children.

III.

Normally a father receives not only love and obedience but also respect. A young child's reaction to the father's voice is different from his response to the mother's. There is a certain awe and even fear of the male parent. Our text makes this same distinction: "the Lord is merciful to them that fear him." Of course, fear means reverence. "The Lord is kind to those who revere him" is another translation. In Proverbs we read:

> "Trust in the LORD with all your heart,
> And rely not on your own understanding;
> In all your ways acknowledge him,
> And he will make straight your paths.
> Be not wise in your own eyes,
> Revere the LORD, and withdraw from evil. . . .
> My Son, despise not the discipline of the LORD,
> And resent not his correction;
> For whom the LORD loves he corrects,
> Even as a father the son in whom he delights."
> (Prov. 3:5-7a, 11-12, G)

Here again we see the relation between the human and the divine Father. Both are to be treated with respect, and both are givers of justice as well as of kindness. There is a virility about a God of judgment, who punishes, as well as about a God who demands justice, kindness, and mercy.

We stand under the providence of God the Father. We have learned something of this providence from our understanding of human fatherhood, and human paternity in turn has been illuminated by divine paternity.

We may symbolize the Fatherhood of God in terms of two hands. If we think for a moment of God as showing both love and justice, grace and law, forgiveness and judgment, perhaps this is what He is saying to our generation:

"You must and shall have deeper fellowship in your social order. You may take it *this* way (stretching out the right hand) or you may take it *this* way (clenching the left fist). If you will hear my Word, you may yet make the great soulless machine of your industrial civilization an instrument for the common good and a bond of fellowship between you; but if not, then I will smash your civilization, and reduce you to a more primitive level of existence, where you must recover the art of fellowship." [3]

God is this kind of a Father. He loves us enough to have given the life of His Son for us, but He does not spare us from evil. He forgives our sins when we are truly repentant. He gives us power to overcome evil with good. He makes us strong when the Word of God remains within us. "If our heart does not condemn us, then we have confidence in approaching God." He is an ever present help in trouble and sustains us in times of trial and tribulation. As we look at the world around us, as we evaluate the power and significance of human fatherhood, as we observe our children and the hope of the generations to come, we are glad that "in everything God works for good with those who love him" (Rom. 8:28, RSV), for "all things are possible with God." (Mark 10:27, RSV)

> "As a father is kind to his children, so the LORD
> is kind to those who revere him." (Ps. 103:13, G)

---

[3] Walter Marshall Horton, *Realistic Theology* (New York: Harper), p. 113. Used by permission of the publisher.

22.

CHRISTIANITY AND COMMUNISM

INDEPENDENCE DAY

PSALM 122; DEUTERONOMY 4:1-14; ACTS 4:32-5:11;

HYMNS 145, 522, 521, 147

> There was not a needy person among them, for as many as were possessors of lands or houses sold them, and brought the proceeds of what was sold and laid it at the apostles' feet; and distribution was made to each as any had need. (Acts 4:34-35, RSV)

This "communism" of the early Church makes it clear that common ownership is not opposed by Christianity. On this day when we thank God for the independence and freedoms of our nation, let us look for a moment at this small, first-century, community, bound together by Christian love, where members who had property *voluntarily* sold all that they had for the benefit of the poorer members.

Ananias and his wife also sold their property, and pretended to give their money to the community, but they held back some of it. The reason Peter excommunicated Ananias was not because he refused to be a communist, but because he lied. "While it remained unsold," said Peter, "did it not remain your own? And after it was sold, was it not at your disposal? How is it that you contrived this deed in your heart? You have not lied to men but to God." (Acts

5:4, RSV) Many other Christians kept their possessions, and made their privately owned houses available for Christian meetings.

The tragedy of this early Christian communism was that it failed and the Jerusalem church was bankrupt, so that Paul had to bring financial aid from the churches outside of Jerusalem.

Against this background, the Archbishop of York said that while this kind of communism is impractical, leads to ruin, and is politically unworkable, it should not be condemned as unchristian. The Lambeth Conference, which includes all our bishops, said that communism was morally neutral and a Christian may well be a communist, but he can not be a Marxian Communist. While this distinction is academic in today's practical politics, it is still important to point up the reasons.

Archbishop Cyril Forster Garbett said, "While it is possible to be a Christian and a Communist, it is not possible to be a Christian and a Marxist Communist without disloyalty either to Christ or to Marx, for Marxian Communism is far more than a political or economic theory; it has a doctrine behind it which leaves no room for Christianity or for any form of theism. It teaches that the world is material; that the material world is the only reality; that the mind is only a product of matter. . . . There can be no common ground between Marxism and Christian doctrine and ethics; they are fundamentally opposed. And the methods of violence, deceit and cruelty used by Communism to gain its ends are the cause of incalculable misery and fear throughout the world. There can be no agreement between militant Communism and a Church which has peace as its aim."[1]

The Lambeth Conference summed up the Anglican position: "Marxian Communism is contrary to Christian faith, for it denies the existence of God, Revelation, and a future life; it treats the

[1] Reported in *Modern Churchman,* Dec. 1948, pp. 332-333; cf. *In An Age of Revolution* (Oxford), pp. 164-166.

individual as a means and not an end; it encourages class warfare; it regards the moral law not as absolute but as relative to the needs of the state." This is not just name-calling, but is based upon the observation of communist beliefs and practices.

Let us see what communism says about Christianity. "Religion," says Lenin, "teaches those who toil in poverty all their lives to be resigned and patient in this world, and consoles them with the hope of reward in heaven. As for those who live upon the labor of others, religion teaches them to be charitable in earthly life, thus providing a cheap justification for their whole exploiting existence and selling them at a reasonable price tickets to heavenly bliss. Religion is the opium of the people. Religion is a kind of spiritual intoxicant, in which slaves of capital drown their humanity and their desires for some sort of decent human existence. . . . We must combat religion—this is the A.B.C. of all materialism, and consequently of Marxism. . . . If a priest joined the Party, and made it his chief and almost exclusive business to propagate religious views, then, of course, the Party would have to expel him. . . . We deny all morality taken from superhuman or non-class conceptions. We say this is a swindle, a befogging of the minds of workers and peasants in the interests of landlords and capitalists. We say that our morality is wholly subordinated to the interests of the class struggle of the proletariat. We deduce our morality from the facts and needs of the class struggle of the proletariat." [2]

These are official statements. They show exactly where communism stands in relation to religion and ethics.

I.

Where, then, lies communism's appeal? Surely it has power to attract large numbers of men and to lead them in the struggle for power.

[2] Lenin, *Religion* (International Publishers), pp. 7, 14, 17.

First, it has an apocalyptic hope that is as compelling as the Christian kingdom of God. It promises a classless world society, in which every man will be completely free from economic and political slavery. It believes that through political and economic strife will come a promised day in which there will be an ideal state. This hope is materialistic, to be sure, but so is capitalism's dream of gadgets for all and plenty for all a materialistic hope.

Second, communism has a message for the forgotten man. We need only to remember the political attractiveness of Franklin Roosevelt's appeal to the common man to become aware of communism's contagion when it promises the common man his full share in an ideal society. By appealing to the largest class, which is the proletariat, communism is speaking to the many who are now among the "have nots" and who see little chance of joining the upper class of the "haves" within any foreseeable future.

Third, communism has a missionary zeal unmatched by any modern enterprise. When one is converted to communism, he knows he has a message which will attract many men. He looks on his communist philosophy as the early Christians looked on the Gospel. Here is something which has to be shared, for only as he draws others into the party will there be a speeding up of the processes of history. It takes men, many men, to create a revolution which will destroy the Church and capitalism, and eliminate the bourgeois class, thus turning the world over to the proletariat.

Finally, communism has faith in the nature of things. The Communist believes implicitly that the processes of history will work out his way. All meanings for life are found in the historical process, and as materialistic processes move from one emphasis to another, the grand solution will come inevitably in terms of the communist state, which is the millennium.

These goals have been encouraged by the failure of Christianity. Christians have not transcended class, race, and national distinctions, and thus communism has a powerful lever among those who are persecuted in such Christian countries as Germany, where Hitler led the slaughter of millions of Jews, and as the United States, where Negroes and other minority groups are denied civil rights and simple justice in many states. Christianity, by aligning itself with the white race and with capitalism, has become so weak in areas where communism's appeal is strong, that communism is now ahead of Christianity in its ability to reach the common people.

II.

Christianity is unalterably opposed to Marxian communism, but what is not often remembered is that capitalism is not Christian either. It is easy to condemn communism, but we need only to remember that capitalism subordinates human needs to profits, produces serious inequalities, makes money more important for judging success than public service, and does nothing to overcome the cycles of mass unemployment. It is no wonder that the voice of the World Church made this statement:

"The Christian churches should reject the ideologies of both Communism and laissez-faire Capitalism, and should seek to draw men away from the false assumption that these extremes are the only alternatives. Each has made promises which it could not redeem. Communist ideology puts the emphasis on economic justice, and promises that freedom will come automatically after the completion of the revolution. Capitalism puts the emphasis on freedom, and promises that justice will follow as a by-product of free enterprise; that, too, is an ideology which has been proved false. It is the responsibility of Christians to seek new, creative solutions which never allow either justice or freedom to destroy the other."[3]

The point to be made is that as Christians we believe that the

[3] *Amsterdam Report,* III, p. 195.

greatest weapon in opposing communism is not capitalism, but Christianity.

III.

The present struggle between Russia and the United States may be conceived as a struggle between communism and capitalism, between Russian imperialism and Vatican politics, between dictatorship and democracy, or between militant atheism and Christian faith. It is only on the basis of Christianity's resources that any of these battles can be decisively won.

But this means putting capitalism and democracy under the judgment of Christianity, and Christianity is more radical in its social implications than many churchmen realize. Christianity stands for all that is good in communism, capitalism, and democracy, but it is critical of their weaknesses.

If Christianity were taken seriously, it would be far more radical than any political plan, and also far more realistic. It would not assume that men are naturally good, and thus would avoid the optimistic delusions which are fundamental assumptions of all secular idealisms, whether in communism, socialism, or capitalism. It would also take seriously the equal value, in the sight of God, of all persons, and therefore it would find a base different from class distinctions, levels of wealth, or racial stock for evaluating political and economic measures.

John C. Bennett, in a great little book on *Christianity and Communism,* says that communism is "a compound of half-truth and positive error," and "as a movement of power is a threat to essential forms of freedom," and therefore "it is a responsibility of Christians to resist its extension in the world."[4] While American power

[4] John C. Bennett, *Christianity and Communism* (New York: The Association Press), p. 9.

may be needed to restrain imperialistic communism, the answer to communism lies not in capitalism or democracy, but in Christianity that offers to men all that communism can promise, all that capitalism can hope for, and all that democracy can believe in—and much more. "I came," says Jesus in the fourth Gospel, "that they may have life, and have it abundantly." (John 10:10, RSV) Man is more than matter, more than a political pawn, more than his money or his social position. "Now are we the sons of God, and it doth not yet appear what we shall be." (I John 3:2, KJ) We are "heirs of God, and joint-heirs with Christ." (Rom. 8:17, KJ) This is the religious answer to communism, and for Christians it is basic. Our responsibility is not primarily to save institutions or nations, but to bring people to Christ, so that all people will find a religious answer which transcends their petty and private and class interests.

"Christ is the world's true Light. . . .
In Christ all races meet,
Their ancient feuds forgetting,
The whole round world complete,
From sunrise to its setting:
When Christ is throned as Lord,
Men shall forsake their fear,
To ploughshare beat the sword,
To pruning-hook the spear." (Hymn 258)

23.

A MAN'S CALLING

LABOR SUNDAY

PSALM 127; ECCLESIASTES 5:8-20; EPHESIANS 4:1-15;

HYMNS 511, 156, 510, 573

> Walk worthy of the vocation wherewith ye are called. (Eph. 4:1, KJ)

A man and his wife were on their way home from Europe and became interested in a young Finnish girl traveling in steerage. She was looking for work, and they decided to offer her a job.

"Can you cook?" they asked.

"No, I can't cook. My mother always did the cooking."

"Can you do the housework, then?"

"No, my oldest sister always did the housework."

"We could let you take care of the children."

"No, I couldn't do that. My youngest sister always took care of the children."

"Perhaps you could do the sewing."

"No, my aunt always did the sewing."

In despair, the couple asked, "Then what can you do?"

The girl was quite bright and cheerful as she replied, "I can milk reindeer." [1]

Most of us are not limited to milking reindeer, but there are

---

[1] From *Thesaurus of Anecdotes,* edited by Edmund Fuller, copyright, 1942, by Crown Publishers. Used by permission of Crown Publishers, Inc.

times when the tasks that we have the opportunity of doing seem almost as insignificant. Some of us look down on our work as something to get out of the way in order to have some precious leisure; others think brainwork is superior to any kind of work with the hands. This is possibly a natural reaction, but it is also an inheritance from the Greeks, who thought philosophers were a superior order of society and artisans a lesser order, with the military in between.

The Christian has always recognized the dignity of work. "Sweet is the sleep of a laborer," wrote an Old Testament preacher. (Eccles. 5:12, RSV) Paul's letters are full of references to work. He was proud of his own work as a tentmaker. He wrote, "Work with your own hands, as we charged you." (I Thess. 4:11, RSV) "If any one will not work, let him not eat. For we hear that some of you are living in idleness, mere busybodies, not doing any work. Now such persons we command and exhort in the Lord Jesus Christ to do their work in quietness and to earn their own living. Brethren, do not be weary in well-doing." (II Thess. 3:10b-13, RSV)

For the Christian, work is an ethical duty and has positive value. "He who prays and labors lifts his heart to God with his hands," as Bernard of Clairvaux wrote. As far as we know, all the early followers of Jesus were laboring men. Jesus and his family shared a carpenter shop. Peter and others were fishermen. Martha kept house. Levi was a tax collector. A rich man provided a grave for Jesus. All the disciples were laymen seeking truth and salvation, and their ministry was supported by their daily work. Paul used to argue in the synagogue on the sabbath, and work during the week. In Corinth, he joined with Aquila and Priscilla and they worked together as tentmakers. There is never any suggestion that work is mere drudgery or ignoble or a necessary evil.

Even milking reindeer is a form of service. In her home in northern Finland, the little girl (later in steerage) had fulfilled her part in family life, even though it hardly prepared her for work in a non-reindeer country. Even she could sing with Studdert-Kennedy:

> "Awake, awake to love and work!
> The lark is in the sky,
> The fields are wet with diamond dew,
> The worlds awake to cry
> Their blessings on the Lord of life,
> As he goes meekly by." (Hymn 156)

I.

The Christian at his work seeks to meet certain standards, and this is probably the most difficult aspect of the concept of vocation. Shakespeare gives us this conversation in *Henry IV:*

"Why, Hal, 'tis my vocation."

To which Hal replies: "'tis no sin for a man to labour in his vocation."[2]

Almost any task may be Christian, provided we keep our eyes on the chief goal, which is the service of our fellows. One of the most deeply Christian men I know is firmly convinced that the greatest service he can render any man is to sell him all the life insurance he can afford. With this conviction, it is no wonder that he heads a large sales organization. When he addresses his salesmen, his words ring with the power of a sermon, and, indeed, he often uses the previous Sunday's sermon as a basis for his talks. He renders this same kind of service to his Church. During the depression, when he lost most of his money, he never cut his substantial pledge to the Church, even though he had to borrow the money to keep up his payments. He feels that he can best serve God and his fellows as a layman who is a great salesman of life insurance.

This element of service is deep-rooted in the Christian concept

---

[2] *Henry IV.* Pt. I. Act I. Sc. 2. L. 116.

of work. It involves a self-giving far beyond the normal demands of routine. A loving mother never measures her service in terms of time spent or of objectives gained. She points beyond all of these. What she seeks is the ultimate good of all her children in terms of what they truly need. We do not serve our job; we do not serve an idea; we serve persons.

> "Go, labor on! spend and be spent!
> Thy joy to do the Father's will:
> It is the way the Master went;
> Shall not the servant treat it still?" (Hymn 573)

Work is also an end in itself. We know what happens among both children and adults when there are idle hands and empty hours. We know what happens to sorrowful hearts when there is no work to fill their emptiness. We know that work has a therapeutic value. Most cases of nervous instability and illness are found among those who have nothing to challenge them.

> "Labor is rest—from the sorrows that greet us;
> Rest from all petty vexations that meet us,
> Rest from sin-promptings that ever entreat us,
> Rest from the world-sirens that hire us to ill.
> Work—and pure slumbers shall wait on thy pillow;
> Work—thou shalt ride over Care's coming billow;
> Lie not down wearied 'neath Woe's weeping willow!
> Work with a stout heart and resolute will."[3]

II.

In Ephesians there is a text for all this: "Walk worthy of the vocation wherewith ye are called." (4:1, KJ) Or as other translators

---

[3] Frances S. Osgood, "To Labor Is to Pray," in Hoyt's *New Cyclopedia of Practical Quotations* (New York: Funk), p. 425.

put it: "Live lives worthy of the summons you have received." (G) "Live a life worthy of your calling." (M)

Here is the idea of vocation, summons, calling. A man's calling is to do the work that God has summoned him to do. If a man is faithful, God will give him grace to use his abilities in a field of service to his fellow beings.

"All service is the same with God,"[4] says Browning. It is not the job we do, but the spirit with which we do it that counts in the end. It is, as Bishop Cumberland says, "better to wear out than to rust out." "All work, even cotton-spinning, is noble," says Carlyle; "work alone is noble."[5]

This is only one-third of our problem. It is good to work. But we face a second aspect of the Christian doctrine of work when we discover that there are unnecessary and unpleasant aspects of many jobs. It is not always possible to find work that serves our fellows. The machine eliminates certain kinds of back-breaking work and substitutes the requirements of an automaton.

There are elements in many jobs and there are jobs in themselves which are rapacious, grasping, selfish, and parasitic on the community. They do more evil than good because of the way they are run or because of their very nature. They may draw to them the unsavory elements of society; they may encourage racketeering; they may depend upon the gambling instinct; or they may simply be unfair to the public.

There are also the mass-production tasks, in which it is hard to realize the service rendered to the community because of the immediate concerns of the worker with the nuts and bolts and the assembly line. There are dangerous tasks that have their rewards, and there are also jobs which seem mere drudgery and in which the element of true service is hard to see.

---

[4] Robert Browning, *Pippa Passes,* Pt. IV.
[5] *Past and Present,* Bk. III, Ch. 4.

III.

In the light of these difficulties, the Christian must seek the meaning of his vocation. Professor Robert Calhoun has suggested that the answer lies in three basic questions:

Is what I am doing truly needful?

Does my job do justice to my own abilities?

Does my work contribute to the betterment of the world?[6]

What needs to be done is a matter of fact. The number needed to accomplish certain tasks is also statistical. These facts are external to a man's personal inclinations, and therefore he must take them into account. The Christian demand is to seek out needed work, so that the service of country and community will be achieved. Too often the motives of pleasure, profit, prestige, and even divine favor become primary, and we forget what Jesus said about being among men as one that serves.

This call to do needful work can be understood only against the background of one's own ability. The unique element in a man's calling is that he has certain native and latent capacities, and whatever he does must be compatible with his aptitudes. Among the possible tasks that are needed for the ongoing processes of society, he must choose within the limitations of his own individual powers.

We can usually see jobs that are needed for which we have some ability within the framework of a secular society. But when we suggest that this needful work be a contribution to the betterment of the common life of the world, we are moving into the realm of high idealism. Within the frameworks of economic competition and nationalistic pride, it is hard to see how any kind of production can rise to the level of true concern for the welfare of mankind. The bigness of corporations and states, the power of government and the restrictions of the police state, the impersonal relations of a society

[1] Robert Calhoun, *God and the Common Life,* pp. 54, 56, 59.

that has outgrown moral standards based on the personal relations of small groups—all of these factors complicate the problem.

It is in such circumstances that we are called by God to walk worthy of the vocation to which we are called. Whether we are to milk reindeer or to be tentmakers, we know that

"All labor gained new dignity
Since he who all creation made
Toiled with his hands for daily bread
Right manfully." (Hymn 510)

So we are called of God to do needful work, to fulfil our own destiny in the light of our capacity, and to contribute to the common welfare.

"The Lord had a job for me, but I had so much to do,
I said, 'You get somebody else—or wait till I get through.'
I don't know how the Lord came out, but He seemed to get along;
But I felt kinda sneakin' like, 'cause I know'd I done Him wrong.
One day I needed the Lord—needed Him myself—needed Him right away,
And he never answered me at all, but I could hear Him say
Down in my accusin' heart, 'I'se got too much to do,
You get somebody else or wait till I get through.' "[7]

[7] Paul Laurence Dunbar, *The Lord Had a Job,* in Hoyt's *New Cyclopedia of Practical Quotations* (New York: Funk), p. 908.

24.

"AND GLADLY TEACH"

RELIGIOUS EDUCATION SUNDAY

PSALM 111; JOB 28:12-28; MATTHEW 18:1-14;

HYMNS 299, 505, 506, 507

The title of this sermon is taken from the autobiography of one of America's foremost teachers: *And Gladly Teach,* by Bliss Perry of Harvard. He, in turn, took his text from Chaucer:

"And gladly wolde he lerne, and gladly teche."

Throughout the Gospels, Jesus is referred to as rabbi, which means teacher. He is an excellent example of the teacher *par excellence.* He won His learners (which is what disciples means) by the winsomeness of His personality, by the attractiveness of what He had to say, by His ability to hold their interest because His message was vital and compelling, by the simple contagion of a way of life that was as catching as a disease, by His informal manner of meeting His learners at their "growing edge." He drew His illustrations from their common life, from their daily experiences, from the roadside, and from nature. He taught them gladly and with abandon, and they gladly learned from Him.

This man Jesus was a rabbi, steeped in the wisdom and traditions of the Jewish religion, able to interpret the law and the prophets, and always throwing new light on what was either taken for granted or forgotten in the Jewish traditions.

He was not always a good fellow, for, while He mixed with the wine-bibbers and the sinners, there were times when His message included scolding and the threat of judgment. He was not afraid of discipline. He never backed down in a disputation, and He was often heckled. In one way, His teaching was like a modern bull session, with questions prompted by the life-centeredness of his teaching. There was nothing dull or routine about all this.

He trained His disciples to be teachers. The great commission at the close of the Gospel according to Matthew attributes these words to Him: "Go therefore and make disciples of all nations . . . teaching them to observe all that I have commanded you." (Matt. 28:19a-20a, RSV)

I.

Bliss Perry describes a contrasting approach in the teaching of Latin. "There were no sections; good, bad, and indifferent students had precisely the same assignments and were called up in turn. We were doing, literally, what our fathers had done before us. My first Latin lesson . . . was, as I discovered later in Father's diary, exactly the same assignment which he had had in 1848; and it was also precisely what my son had at Williams as a freshman in 1916. For sixty-eight years, at least, and probably much longer, it was the same squirrel in the same cage! One would think that some Professor of Latin, at some time, in an access of emotional insanity might have altered the assignment, even if he kept the dreadful secret to himself." [1]

Of course, that is no worse than teaching the Bible by beginning with Genesis. It is no worse than many of our theologies that imply that to be a Christian one must jump through specific intellectual hoops. We have gone a long way from the sterile and unimaginative teaching of a century ago. We are returning to the techniques

[1] Bliss Perry, *And Gladly Teach* (Boston: Houghton Mifflin, 1935), p. 38. Used by permission.

of the greatest Teacher of all, who, long before the days of John Dewey, began His lessons with the needs of His particular pupils in mind.

Therefore, what we have to say applies to all of us, and not just to church school teachers, Christian teachers in public schools, and parents. To be a Christian is to teach. Every mother teaches, every missionary teaches, every churchman teaches. It is simply a question of whether it is good or bad teaching.

II.

A book called *Great Teachers* includes such giants as Mark Hopkins, Woodrow Wilson, William James, John Dewey, Cesar Franck, and Sigmund Freud. At the conclusion of many fascinating chapters, there is this comment: "While good teaching will differ widely in its methods, there is at least one thing in which all good teaching will be alike: no teaching is good which does not arouse and 'dephlegmatize' the students, . . . which does not engage as its allies their awakened, sympathetic, and co-operating faculties." [2]

A teacher cannot assume that his class will share his interest in his subject. To him, it may be fascinating, but it may seem to the students to be routine or dull or beyond their ken. Here is the Bible, which is the most interesting and vital set of books in the history of the world, but it is hard to sell to Johnny "Hot-Rod," or to Mary "Doll-Lover," or to Mrs. "Stick-in-the-Mud," or to Mr. "Harassed Business Man." Missionary heroes are brave and courageous souls, but they may seem unexciting compared with the fourth grader's discovery of a new hero on television. Church history is a commentary on Western civilization, but high school students may find juke box serenades more relevant to their needs. All of this is related to teaching, to the personality of the teacher, and to the achievement of a common interest.

---

[2] Houston Peterson (ed.), *Great Teachers* (New Brunswick: Rutgers Univ. Press), p. 341.

A student sometimes falls asleep in class. In one instance where this happened, the boy recovered consciousness after having called attention to himself by his snores, and he blurted out an apology. "No," said the professor, "it is I who should apologize to you for not keeping you awake."[3] This may seem obvious enough, but such an apology shook the ivy clad walls of that college. In the Book of Acts there is a similar incident, when Paul was preaching. "A young man named Eutychus, who was sitting at the window, became very drowsy as Paul's address grew longer and longer, and finally went fast asleep and fell from the third story to the ground, and was picked up for dead. But Paul went downstairs, and threw himself upon him, and put his arms around him.

"'Do not be alarmed,' he said, 'he is still alive.'

"Then he went upstairs again, and broke bread, and ate, and after a long talk with them that lasted until daylight, he went away. They took the boy home alive, and were greatly comforted." (Acts 20:9-12, G)

Jesus never had this trouble. The reason He had to find food for the five thousand was because they were so interested in His teaching that they forgot to go home. The story is told of Reinhold Niebuhr, one of America's foremost theologians, that while he was giving the Gifford Lectures at Edinburgh, there was a slight uneasiness among his listeners. Niebuhr, in his brilliant way, put on more steam to recapture their interest. Afterward, he inquired of a friend why there was this momentary lapse, and the friend replied, "While you were talking, we had the first air-raid alarm of the war."

The most needed trait in any teacher is the Christian virtue of radiance. A contagious enthusiasm for the subject is the most effective way of capturing interest, but it is something that cannot be feigned. No one can convert a friend to Christianity unless he has in his own personality a certain radiance. So it is with all teaching.

---

[3] *Ibid.*, p. 341.

"But there he was; a strong man talking with knowledge and a sort of dark enthusiasm: and sentence by sentence he enforced a high contagion."[4]

A high contagion must be aimed at the right level. We need to catch our learners, our new disciples, our potential converts, at their growing edge. The enthusiasm of the teacher must be a combination of contagious interest in his subject and loving concern for his pupils.

For Christianity this combination of contagion and concern for the pupil operates within a community. Because both the teacher and the pupil are equally the subjects of a loving God within the framework of the Church, they recognize the need for redemption. The Church at its best is a redemptive and redeeming community, and Christian education takes place when both teacher and pupil are alert to the redemptive processes of God in their midst. The Christian faith is communicated within the framework of a community of faith and grace.

So the Christian teacher has three concerns: a passionate regard for the truth of Christianity, a loving consideration of the needs of his learner, and a concern that both of them will be the recipients of God's grace within the community of faithful people where the word of God is truly preached and the sacraments are duly administered. In the last analysis, it is God who makes possible the acceptance of the saving knowledge of Christ which is offered in a curriculum of Christian education.

III.

Because Christianity is a joyous and rich experience, the response to the contagion of Christian faith is that our disciples will "gladly lerne."

There is no learning until there are attention and reaction. Only

---

[4] *Ibid.*, p. 342.

as students are "de-phlegmatized" is there any real learning. Socrates called himself a gadfly, because he conceived his task to be to talk men to truth through forcing them to think for themselves. Plato's students wrestled with his great dialogues, which presented all sides of a question. Amos thundered that man should hunger and thirst after righteousness. In them we find consecrated teaching, because the listeners responded, not always favorably of course, to the truth which is God's gift to men.

"For Socrates who, phrase by phrase,
Talked men to truth, unshrinking,
And left for Plato's mighty grace
To mold our ways of thinking;
For all who wrestled, sane and free,
To win the unseen reality,
To God be thanks and glory." (Hymn 299, stanza 3)

To make Christianity dull and uninteresting is one of the greatest crimes of the church schools. Of such Christians, we can say with Thomson about the linnets, who

"... sit
On the dead tree, a dull despondent flock."[5]

All of us are Christian teachers. We are good teachers if we love God enough and His children enough, for then we shall take the pains to find the techniques of transferring what we know to the meaningful relations of life. As a Christian, each of us is commissioned to go and teach all nations, make disciples of all the heathen, make learners of all men. We are to help fulfil the prediction, "You will know the truth, and the truth will make you free." (John 8:32, RSV) We are here to put before men the challenge: "I am the way, the truth, and the life." (John 14:6, KJ) We are to educate our children, our neighbors, our friends, or anyone else who will

---

[5] James Thomson, *The Seasons. Autumn.* L. 974.

listen. The second letter to Timothy sums it up: "Preach the word, be urgent in season and out of season, convince, rebuke, and exhort, be unfailing in patience and in teaching." (II Timothy 4:2, RSV)

There is a famous phrase in the Book of Acts, in which King Agrippa says to Paul: "Almost thou persuadest me to be a Christian." (Acts 26:28, KJ) But this is not a correct translation, and Paul was not a failure as a teacher. What Agrippa really said was, "You are in a hurry to persuade me and make a Christian of me." (G) The "almost persuaded" leads to tragedy:

> "Almost persuaded, now to believe;
> Almost persuaded, Christ to receive; . .
> Almost but lost!"[6]

Paul went right to the point: "King Agrippa, do you believe the prophets? I know that you do!" (Acts 26:27, G) If Paul could so challenge a king, then we can run the gauntlet before the people we know in every walk of life. The last point is always "thou"—"you!" That is Christian teaching.

---

[6] Quoted by Halford Luccock, *The Acts of the Apostles* (New York: Harper), II, 161.

25.

THE ECUMENICAL REFORMATION

WORLD-WIDE COMMUNION SUNDAY

(EPISTLE AND GOSPEL): I CORINTHIANS 1:10-15; JOHN 17:20-25;

HYMNS 557, 191, 211, 396

> I . . . pray . . . that they may all be one, . . . so that the world may believe that thou hast sent me. (John 17:21, RSV)

These words ascribed to Jesus in the fourth Gospel are the motivation for Christian unity. On World-Wide Communion Sunday, when Christians of whatever name receive the sacrament of Holy Communion in their own ways, we rejoice in the unity that already exists, and we are repentant before the ideal of the prayer for unity. We rejoice in the hope for further unity, and we are sorrowful that many barriers still face us.

Presiding Bishop Henry Knox Sherrill puts it this way: "The World Council of Churches is still largely an ideal held by many of the leaders of the Churches. It has not yet touched the lives of the overwhelming majority of clergy and of laity. This whole movement must be brought to the parochial level in a great program of education. On the one hand we must promote this ideal in every possible way, by means of popular education and of enthusiastic report. On the other hand there is danger that we give the impression that we have already reached an objective which is in reality still distant."[1]

In this twentieth century, a new word has come across the Church's horizon. It is really an old word, for the Greeks had a word for it. The word is *ecumenical* and it means world-wide, or "the science of the world-Christian community." For example, with the coming of the era of global unity as marked by the airplane and the radio, when all men became neighbors whether they liked it or not, the German philosopher Keyserling began to speak of an ecumenical era.

The term ecumenical has been applied to the Church since the earliest councils, because these councils drew representatives of the Church from throughout the known world. The term dropped out of use after a number of councils were held, and did not reappear until the twentieth century. Beginning in 1910, Churches of the non-Roman persuasion began to come together in the search for unity. This movement has had so profound an effect upon the Churches that Robert Bilheimer has written of *The Ecumenical Reformation* as the turning point of modern Christianity.[2]

This ecumenical reformation means that all communions will cooperate in their allegiance to Jesus Christ. It means to believe in "the holy, Catholic Church" as somehow in existence when the Churches mutually recognize each other as valid Churches.

I.

To see this movement in proper perspective, we need to remember that there has never been a united Church. We have tended to romanticize and glamorize the early and medieval Church, when

---

[1] Henry Knox Sherrill, *The Church's Ministry in Our Time* (New York: Scribner), p. 53. Used by permission of the publisher.

[2] Robert S. Bilheimer, *What Must the Church Do?* (New York: Harper), pp. 63-107.

all Christians were supposed to have been under one roof, but they were not united.

In New Testament times, Paul had to fight for unity against those who cried, "'I belong to Paul,' or 'I belong to Apollos,' or 'I belong to Cephas,' or 'I belong to Christ.' Is Christ divided?" (I Cor. 1:12-13a, RSV) At the council of Jerusalem, Paul was the central figure in the controversy over whether Gentiles could be admitted to the Church without first becoming Jews through circumcision. Paul believed in unity, but he always had to fight for it. There never was an undivided Church. Little groups were constantly breaking off from the main stream of the Christian tradition. They did not always endure for long, but they were permanent breaks in the body of Christ.

At every one of the so-called ecumenical councils between A.D. 325 and A.D. 1054, the ideal of unity was confirmed by expelling some group from the Church. The famous council of Nicea was attended by only a fraction of the bishops. While an early form of the Nicene Creed was approved, disputes broke out again almost immediately. To show how unsettled this period was, we need only to remember that Athanasius, who was victorious at Nicea, was banished from his bishopric five times in the next fifty years.

The Council of Ephesus in 431 drove out the Nestorians. Many independent groups of today, including the Armenian Christians, the Coptic Churches, the Jacobites, and the Malabar Christians in India, were driven out of the Catholic Church in 451 at the Council of Chalcedon.

Some people would like to make these councils the basis for Christian unity today. Among the requirements were: clerics are forbidden to lend money at interest, candidates for bishop's orders must know the Psalter by heart, no church is to be consecrated without relics, women must not dwell in bishops' houses.

For eighteen centuries, the Church has affirmed unity in prin ciple, whereas the life of the Church has been marked by a steady succession of divisions and schisms. The process of division was stepped up with the Reformation, and did not begin to slow down until about a century ago. But there has been a change in direction. No longer do we merely talk about unity. There is an ecumenical reformation which points to a reunion of Christendom.[3]

II.

The newness and freshness of this movement mark it as significant. Archbishop Temple, one of the greatest leaders produced by the movement, wrote:

"As though in preparation for such a time as this, God has been building up a Christian fellowship which now extends into almost every nation, and binds citizens of them all together in true unity and mutual love. No human agency has planned this. It is the result of the great missionary enterprise of the last hundred and fifty years. Neither the missionaries nor those who sent them out were aiming at the creation of a world-wide fellowship interpenetrating the nations, bridging the gulfs between them, and supplying the promise of a check to their rivalries. The aim for nearly the whole period was to preach the Gospel to as many individuals as could be reached, so that those who were won to discipleship should be put in the way of eternal salvation. Almost incidentally the great world-fellowship has arisen; it is the great new fact of our era; it makes itself apparent from time to time in World Conferences such as in the last twenty years have been held in Stockholm, Lausanne, Jerusalem, Oxford, Edinburgh, Madras, Amsterdam."[4]

These words by Archbishop Temple were part of his enthrone-

---

[3] See Henry P. Van Dusen, *World Christianity*, pp. 67-71, for these facts in detail.

[4] William Temple, *The Church Looks Forward* (New York: Macmillan, 1944), p. 2. Used by permission of the publisher.

ment sermon as Archbishop of Canterbury. This is his ideal for the Anglican Communion and for the ecumenical reformation.

On this World-Wide Communion Sunday, we need to pray,

"For all thy Church, O Lord, we intercede;
Make thou our sad divisions soon to cease;
Thus may we all one bread, one body be,
Through this blest sacrament of unity." (Hymn 191, stanza 2)

While this is the ideal, the goal is far off. The Roman Church is not part of the movement. When Bishop Parsons and others visited the Pope in 1919, they were received graciously and had a pleasant visit, but the Holy Father said that the only way there could be Church unity was on Rome's terms, that they "should submit themselves to the one whom their Lord had appointed to be their rightful head, the one to whom they were then speaking. It is reported that when the delegation was returning from their visit to Rome, the Anglo-Catholic member of the delegation, the Bishop of Fond du Lac, remained silent for some time. Then raising his hand to heaven he shook his fist three times and expressed his judgment on the attitude of the Bishop of Rome in terms which were more forceful than complimentary."[5] Our ecumenical reformation is limited to non-Roman Churches not by our choice but by Roman decision.

There are other difficulties. A group of Anglicans at the great Ecumenical Institute in Switzerland refused to receive Communion when the service was celebrated by the great Dutch leader, Dr. Visser 't Hooft, thus breaking the spell at the close of an otherwise inspiring meeting. At a previous conference, a Southern Baptist could not in good conscience receive Communion from the hands

[5] William Adams Brown, *Toward a United Church* (New York: Scribner), p. 60.

of the Archbishop of Canterbury because the latter had not been properly immersed.

In spite of these episodes, the direction today is toward closer unity and has been for forty years. The great missionary movements, educational enterprises, Bible societies, and other special functions have required cooperation. The increasing federation, as exemplified in the great conferences and in the National and World Councils of Churches, symbolizes the unity that already exists. Above all, there have been many mergers of Churches, the most dramatic of which is the Church of South India, which crosses several denominational and traditional lines.

Individual Christians tend to cross denominational lines, and often they feel more at home in Churches not of their own inheritance. President Van Dusen gives us a picture of the situation: "A Broad Church Episcopalian finds himself more at home among liberal Presbyterians of the same cultural outlook than among 'spikey' Anglo-Catholics or fellow-Episcopalians of a different social stratum. A 'fundamentalist' Baptist is far closer to 'fundamentalist' Methodists than to fellow-Baptists who have drunk deep of Modernist Humanism. Everywhere in the world, Protestants of any Communion will be found gravitating to a church of their own nationality and language, whatever its denomination, rather than to a church of their own Communion which worships in unfamiliar speech. These facts cast a revealing searchlight upon the actualities of Christian division and upon the unrealities of most denominational demarcations." [6]

III.

Statistics and catalogs do not catch fire in the hearts of men, but they undergird our vision and supply a realistic view of what is

[6] Henry P. Van Dusen, *What IS the Church Doing?* (New York: Scribner), pp. 164-165. Used by permission of the publisher.

happening in the Church. We believe in "one, holy, Catholic, Apostolic Church." The only place where this Church exists is in the ecumenical movement, for this provides the world-wide Christian community which is universal in its scope and orthodox in its beliefs. Only through this world-wide Christian community can there be one Church; only as Christians come together in unity can the Church be holy; only as the Church is universal or ecumenical can it be catholic; and only as we try to catch the vision of unity held by the apostles are we in their fellowship.

Bishop Parsons writes: "If God as revealed in Christ is love, the Church which carries the good tidings of that revelation to the world must be one. A divided Church is repudiating the very Gospel it proclaims. It is imperiling the witness to the truth in Christ. The great prayer of St. John 17, whether a report of the Lord's words or not, certainly opens to us his mind. 'That they may all be one, . . . that the world may know that thou didst send me.' That this means a visible unity is obvious. If what is often spoken of as spiritual unity really exists, visible unity is inevitable." [7]

This is not a question of regimentation. No Church needs to worry about losing its beloved traditions. Episcopalians will keep their Prayer Book and their bishops. But this is not the issue. As long as Christians of any persuasion keep themselves aloof from the whole body of Christ, they are setting up barriers to the practice of Christian love.

There are a few things we can do about this right now. Beginning on the local level, each one of us can find ways to support the work of the local Council of Churches, for these councils promote the Gospel through education, cooperative social service,

---

[7] Edward L. Parsons, in *Christianity and the Contemporary Scene,* ed. by Randolph C. Miller and Henry H. Shires (New York: Morehouse-Gorham), p. 101. Used by permission of the publisher.

community worship, and in many other ways. On a broader level, we need to know about state councils of Churches, through which our Christian concerns are made known to the government and our special conferences provide a platform for our common Christian conscience. On the national level, the National Council of Churches brings together the concerns of all the Churches in the areas where cooperation is deemed desirable. And beyond that there is the World Council of Churches, which Archbishop Temple called "the great new fact of our era." We need to explore the ways in which consecrated lay people can support these great movements toward the "visible catholicity" of all the Churches, for "the Church has never been Catholic enough."[8]

We need to pray with our Lord that all Christians may be one. We need to thank God that in the last fifty years there has been an ecumenical reformation which is fanning the flames of the hopes for unity and that, therefore, there is hope for the Church and for the world.

---

[8] *Ibid.*, p. 114.

26.

"THE DAYS OF THY YOUTH"

YOUTH SUNDAY

PSALM 121; ECCLESIASTES 12:1-17; MATTHEW 25:31-46;

HYMNS 509, 508, 505, 531

> Rejoice, O young man, in your youth,
> And let your mind be glad in the days of your vigor. . . .
> Remember your Creator in the days of your vigor,
> Before the evil days come,
> And the years approach of which you will say,
> 'I have no pleasure in them.' . . .
> On the day when the . . .
> . . . spirit returns to God who gave it.
> (Eccles. 11:9; 12:1, 3, 7, G)

The old cynic who wrote that "all is vanity" was a very mature man. He was seeking to find out why life is worth living. He did not see very much around him to make him happy. He saw that people who lived without God were not wise or happy or able to make life worth living. So all is vanity when one relies on his own power to find happiness. Even if one only wants to eat and drink and enjoy life, he cannot do it—unless he has faith in God.

Throughout the book of Ecclesiastes, the preacher is seeking to find life's meaning. He ardently yearns for some key to the puzzle, and he falls back on his familiar refrain, "all is vanity." As a man grows old, his body falls apart. In his final chapter, he compares the vigor of youth with the ravages of old age. He uses poetic symbols to describe what happens as a man's hearing and eyesight get poorer, as his hair gets gray, his vocal chords get scratchy, and his glands refuse to function adequately. So the body falls apart, and then "the dust returns to the earth." It is a sad picture, until his last line: "and the spirit returns to God who gave it!" (12:7, RSV)

If this is the end of life, it becomes obvious that we can find the meaning of life only by rejecting false views. If you think you can be happy by eating and drinking, says the preacher, get the idea out of your head, for when you grow old what fun is eating when you have a sour stomach? If you think money and possessions are what give life its meaning, stop thinking that way, for all is vanity and nothing will be left.

There is only one answer. When we have the wisdom of God, we find meaning in life. Here is the answer: "Let us hear the conclusion of the whole matter: Fear God, and keep his commandments: for this is the whole duty of man." (Eccles. 12:13, KJ)

I.

What does this mean for young people today? When should we start to learn what the old man has to tell us? The whole conclusion of the preacher is to the point:

> "Remember also thy Creator in the days of thy youth. . . .
> "Rejoice, O young man, in thy youth, and let thy heart cheer thee in the days of thy youth." (12:1, 11:9, ASV)

Youth is an expensive and tortuous operation. It is not easy to grow up. Think what it costs society to bring a boy through the educational system. It costs about thirty-six hundred dollars to get a boy through the eighth grade. High school costs at least another twenty-five hundred dollars, and if he goes to college it costs four thousand dollars more. When you add the figures of what the community, state, and nation spend for his protection and other special services, the total mounts to about twenty-five thousand dollars. In addition to what a youth owes his parents, there is this twenty-five thousand dollar debt to the world when he grows up.

Have you ever thought of yourself as a twenty-five thousand dollar investment? Society has put that much into you, and what is the return on its investment? What are you worth to your family, your school, your community, your nation?

We must have a lot of faith in our youth, or we would not spend that much money on them.

What kind of a return do we want? "To sum it all up, in conclusion," says the preacher, "stand in awe of God, obey his orders: that is everything, for every man." (12:13, M)

This begins when we rejoice in our youth. When we remember our Creator, we behave in the way God wants. It is not a matter of age, really, for many young men pay off their obligation to society in full at an early age.

I am thinking of such a boy, a boy who fulfilled his goals with rejoicing, who remembered his Creator, and who faced death with the assurance that "the spirit returns to God who gave it." He stands as a shining example of what a Christian man ought to be. In his relations with his Church where he was a loyal member of the servers' and young peoples' groups after having come up through the church school, in his relations with his family where he was a loving son and brother, in his popularity among his many friends in school and later in the Army, he was an example of integrity that grew to the sure serenity of faith as he reached maturity in the midst of suffering and the approach of death. He faced death without fear and with unfailing confidence. I was with him before he died, and I could see the peace of God reflected in his face, in his attitude, and in his words. Because he knew God in his youth, Richard Warrington faced God with serenity as he moved into a new and richer life with God.

I wish I could impress on all of you the significance of Christian faith. I know what happens to a man when he sees his world crumbling all around him. But God is the real foundation from now to eternity, just because He is always present, always available, always ready to lift us from blind despair to the confident hope of faith.

When the preacher could not find a meaning in life without God, he went through all the possibilities. And there simply is nothing else to rely on. If we put our faith in wealth, moth and rust can corrupt it. When we put our faith in our friends, they die or fade away. When we put our faith in the nation, governments change and nations fall. When we put our faith in anything that we do, we discover that the end is vanity. "Utterly vain—such is the Speaker's verdict—everything is vain!" (12:8, M)

But God is a moving and mysterious presence. We are never far from Him, nor He from us. When we turn from Him, He is always seeking to draw us back into the circle of His love. When we disobey Him, He is willing to forgive us. When we are in trouble, He is the only one who can straighten us out. When we lose our loved ones, He comforts us and gives us the promise of eternal life.

Even the cynical old preacher discovered this. "Obeying his orders" is the ultimate test. This will be judged by God Himself in time, "for in judging all life's secrets, God will have every single thing before him, to decide whether it is good or evil." (12:14, M)

II.

This is exactly what Jesus tells us in one of His most remarkable passages. He says that God will set the sheep on one hand and the goats on the other. And the evil

"shall depart to eternal punishment,
and the just to eternal life." (Matt. 25:46, M)

We obey God, He tells us, by our actions toward our fellows.

"I tell you truly, in so far as you did it to one
of these my brothers, you did it to me." (Matt. 25:40, M)

So we are to feed the hungry, refresh the thirsty, entertain the resident aliens and strangers, clothe those in need, take care of the sick, and visit those in prison. We are to have the same concern for those whom we do not know as we would show for Christ Himself.

We are never too young or too old to start worshiping and obeying God. If we obey God in the days of our youth, we will never be disillusioned, because there is nothing that life can do to us. We have an armor of faith that the arrows of this world cannot pierce. We have interior resources that can take the place of external delights. We have faith in God, and "God is not mocked." We can say with Paul: "I can do anything through God who gives me strength."

This kind of faith, beginning when we are young, leads to a happy life. It gives us a life with meaning. For we know that there is a twenty-five thousand dollar investment in us and that God also made the investment of the life and death of Jesus Christ in each and every one of us. He is the Christ who came that we "might have life, and have it in abundance."

So the Christian, whether he is young or old, reflects the radiance of the glory of Christ. The Christian has an inner serenity that serves him when the road is hard and long. The Christian knows that his spirit will return to God who gave it and, therefore, that nothing can crush his spirit in this world. The Christian is courageous and brave, and his step is poised and sure because he knows that God will lift him up.

We will make the most of our youth, then, because in the joyous use of all that youth affords, we will go from strength to strength in the life of perfect service.

"The Lord shall preserve thee from all evil; yea, it is even he that shall keep thy soul." (Ps. 121:7, PB)

27.

OUR REFORMATION HERITAGE

REFORMATION DAY

PSALM 130; HABBAKUK 2:1-14; ROMANS 5:1-11; HYMNS 551, 446, 524, 538

> Therefore, since we are justified by faith, we have peace with God through our Lord Jesus Christ. Through him we have obtained access to this grace in which we stand, and we rejoice in our hope of sharing the glory of God. (Rom. 5:1-2, RSV)

When Paul wrote these words, he was concerned with those who believed they could be saved by keeping the Law. He saw that no one could keep the Law, and the only way out of the situation was through the grace which God gives freely to those who have faith.

When Martin Luther read these words some fifteen hundred years later, he was concerned with those who believed they could be saved by doing penance or even by buying indulgences. He saw the rottenness of a commercialized system of salvation, and he called men back to faith in God. His study of Paul's letter to the Romans convinced him that men are justified by faith, and not by anything that they do.

As he was teaching his students, he insisted upon the supreme authority of the Bible, and we can see this by a brief look at a class scene from David Evans' radio play, *A Mighty Fortress:*

Luther: "And so, students, we must ever keep in mind that the Bible is our supreme authority; as the house is to the man, the nest to the bird, the stream to the fish, so is Holy Scripture to the believing soul."

First student: "Then, Herr Professor Luther, are we to assume from what you said in this lecture, that the Bible is the supreme authority for Christians?"

Luther: "That was my intention."

First student: "Is this to say, then, that the Church is not our authority?"

Luther: "Let me make my position clear. The Church has the right to speak with a voice of authority, only as it interprets the Scriptures correctly."

Second student: "Then, Herr Professor Luther, does it follow that each individual believer can interpret the Scriptures whichever way he wants to?"

Luther: "Of course not. He will be guided by the Bible, by the Church, and by the Holy Spirit."

Second student: "But this may lead to heresy. If everyone, as you say, has the right of private judgment."

Luther: "Call it what you will. God has given the individual man a conscience which he must respect and follow. When he truly listens to the voice of God speaking through his conscience, he may be led into new ways of discovering God's truth."

Second student: "But no ordinary person is capable of doing so."

Luther: "We must respect the rights of the individual, because he is a child of God. Otherwise, there can be no progress. This is not heresy. This is true Christianity."

The discussion continues until finally a student is completely shocked by this seeming attack on the authority of the Church, and he asks: "Are you not bordering on heresy, sir?"

Luther replies: "Rome is the heretic! I am the true Catholic!"

Such teaching as this, followed by his attack on indulgences, leads finally to his condemnation, for he says:

"I do not recognize any man as head of the Church, but Jesus Christ only, who is the true Rock and Foundation of the Church."

At his trial, he says,

"I neither can, nor will, recant anything. Here I stand. I cannot do otherwise. God help me."

He was protected by German nobles after he was condemned to death, and he was able to provide the leadership which made possible a reformed Church. The Reformation movement traveled rapidly throughout Germany. Under Zwingli and Calvin, it developed in other European countries, and finally, by a twist of the King's marital difficulties, the Reformation reached England.

I.

The Reformation was at work in England long before Henry VIII knew about it. Even when Wycliffe was translating the Bible into English a hundred years before, there was a Protestant movement going back to the Bible for its inspiration. Although Tyndale was forced to flee from Henry VIII, when Tyndale began translating the Bible and adding marginal comments unfavorable to Rome, there were others in England who were in sympathy with the Protestants on the continent. But no strong leadership could grow up in a country dominated by the king. There was no Luther, but a Luther would not have prevailed against Henry in any case, nor could a Calvin or a Zwingli. The political and marital difficulties of Henry brought a break with Rome, and then England's own kind of leadership emerged in the persons of Cranmer, Latimer, Ridley, and others.

We know that there was a close relationship between the English and continental reformers. Cranmer was in Germany long enough to marry the daughter of a German theologian, and he had contact with and was greatly impressed by the great reformers. There was a good deal of correspondence between them, and a continental reformer named Martin Bucer became a professor at Cambridge and was influential in the revision of the Prayer Book of 1552.

The Lutheran influence can be traced most directly in the Articles of Religion. Some of the articles are taken verbatim from Lutheran formularies, and others are modified to suit the English mind and political situation. In every case, the errors of Rome are dispensed with.

Thus, Lutheranism and Anglicanism from the beginning were "protestant" against all errors, and they reformed the Church in terms of the authority of Scripture, "which containeth all things necessary to salvation." Both Cranmer and Luther claimed that in reforming the Church they were true Catholics. They kept as much as was good in Catholicism, with Anglicanism keeping more than Lutheranism. But both kept the sacraments and held much the same view of the Lord's Supper. Both kept an ordered service of worship, with a high liturgical sense. The chief difference was that the Lutherans (except in Sweden) did not keep the historic episcopate.[1]

II.

Three important emphases of the Reformation speak to us today: (1) the authority of Scripture, (2) justification by faith, and (3) Christ is received in the Lord's Supper by faith.

The authority of scripture undercut the Roman view that tradition was of equal authority. The Church's authority is limited to what can be proved by scripture. "Holy Scripture containeth all things necessary to salvation," says the Articles of Religion: "so that whatsoever is not read therein, nor may be proved thereby, is not to be required of any man." While Luther gave more place to the individual conscience and Anglicanism gave more place to the

[1] Powel Mills Dawley, *Chapters in Church History* (Greenwich: The Seabury Press), pp. 136-142; Massey H. Shepherd, Jr., *The Worship of the Church* (Greenwich: The Seabury Press), pp. 68, 88.

opinions of the group, this emphasis on scripture was a middle position between Romish exaltation of tradition and the Anabaptist emphasis on individual inspiration. It provided a rule for the reformed Church of England that is a guide for the modern Christian. As we come to understand the Bible as a record of the mighty acts of God in history, we find new depths of faith and hope in the midst of a world in turmoil.

Justification by faith was in sharp contrast to the Roman view that a believer can be justified by works and that one's merits can get him into heaven. Luther saw the Roman doctrine at work at its lowest level, where people could buy indulgences and could ride on the merits of the saints. They could even gain credit for doing more than God asked of them as a storehouse for future sins. So Anglicans joined Luther and Paul in saying that "we are accounted righteous before God, only for the merit of our Lord and Saviour Jesus Christ by Faith, and not by our own works and deservings," as the Articles of Religion phrases it, adding "we are justified by Faith only." No man is good enough to deserve the salvation proffered by God, but "if we confess our sins, he is faithful and just to forgive us our sins, and to cleanse us from all unrighteousness." (I John 1:9, KJ)

This view combatted the worldly teachings of the Roman Church in the sixteenth century, getting at the worst of the evils of the medieval Church. It serves also as a reminder to us today that we are not measured by being ethical as such, but are made upright and are treated as righteous before God only through faith. The answer to the good man who is not a Christian is that goodness is not enough, even when one is a Christian. Perhaps Luther overdid the emphasis of faith as against works because he saw clearly the low spiritual level of the Roman Church of his time, and Anglicans have tended to modify his position by saying that while good works cannot put away our sins, "yet are they pleasing and acceptable unto God in Christ, and do spring out necessarily of a true and lively faith; insomuch that by them a lively Faith may be as evidently known as a tree discerned by its fruit."

"For by grace you have been saved through faith; and this is not your own doing, it is the gift of God." (Eph. 2:8, RSV)

Faith in relation to the Lord's Supper removed all possibilities of magic from the interpretation of Holy Communion. Luther retained the word, "Mass," but Anglicans preferred the Biblical term, "Lord's Supper," or "Holy Communion." Both rejected the Roman doctrine of transubstantiation, and insisted that Christ was present in the Supper in a spiritual manner to those who were faithful. The lay people were expected to communicate, in both kinds. Noncommunicating masses were forbidden.

The sacrament of Holy Communion indicates God's good will toward us, and is an effectual sign of grace, by which we are strengthened and refreshed. Christ "is present at every celebration of the Supper, present in His risen, life-giving Spirit, sacramentally in the Bread and Wine. In this action we 'remember' Him not only in His Cross and Passion, but also in His mighty Resurrection and Ascension. United to His Person, we are in a wonderful way lifted up into the heavenly places where He is Lord of all."[2]

III.

We have a great Reformation heritage in the Church. We are products of the Catholic tradition, and we are products of the Protestant tradition. We are the most comprehensive Church in Christendom when we remember our dual heritage. And because of the special genius of Anglicanism for including the Greek spirit as handed down through the Renaissance and expressed in freedom of

---

[2] Massey H. Shepherd, Jr., *The Worship of the Church* (Greenwich: The Seabury Press), p. 145.

thought, this comprehensiveness is maintained without the sharp tensions between Catholic and Protestant thought.

On this "Reformation Sunday" we recall in particular the great debt we owe to the courageous and able and devoted Martin Luther, whose Biblical faith started all this. It was he, more than any of the other great reformers, who led the Church away from the errors of Rome. We need the kind of faith that made Luther a great Christian as we sing with him:

> "Did we in our own strength confide,
> Our striving would be losing;
> Were not the right man on our side,
> The man of God's own choosing:
> Dost ask who that may be?
> Christ Jesus, it is he;
> Lord Sabaoth his Name,
> From age to age the same,
> And he must win the battle." (Hymn 551)

"Therefore, since we are justified by faith, we have peace with God through our Lord Jesus Christ. Through him we have obtained access to this grace in which we stand, and we rejoice in our hope of sharing the glory of God." (Rom. 5:1-2, RSV)

28.

"THEY WON THEIR RECORD FOR FAITH"

ALL SAINTS' DAY

PSALM 112; ECCLESIASTES 44:1-15; HEBREWS 11:32-12:2

or (EPISTLE AND GOSPEL) REVELATION 7:2-4, 9-17; MATTHEW 5:1-12;

HYMNS 126, 243, 195, 432

One of the great stories of the Old Testament is the escape of the Hebrews from Egypt. Throughout Israel's history, it stands out as an example of Yahweh's concern for His people. No matter how badly things were going in Israel, the memory of the Exodus was enough to revive their spirits. In the Psalms and other devotions of the Temple, references to crossing the Red Sea were plentiful.

The story is seemingly a simple one. The sea parted to let the Hebrews through and then came back together to drown the Egyptians. But further analysis shows that the present story is a combination of three sources. There is a mixture of history and legend, plus some doubtful geography. The earliest source presents Yahweh working through natural causes, while the later source brings in supernatural elements.

We cannot trace the exact line of Moses' march from Egypt to the desert. The waters have changed their course since then, and one city formerly on the sea is now six miles inland. Some of the northern lakes were formerly connected with the Red Sea. They are now known as Lake Timsah, or the Bitter Lakes. These lakes were shallow and could be crossed by a shallow ford.

It is unlikely that Moses would have led his people to an impassable and deep sea and then counted on a miracle. He was taking enough risk when he left the main traveled road and cut across the shallow waters. The Israelites were traveling light and could ford the water without difficulty, while the Egyptians were riding in heavy chariots and would get stuck in the mud.

The situation was serious. When the people saw water in front of them and the Egyptians chasing them behind, they began to murmur against Moses for getting them into this mess.

"Better to serve the Egyptians than die in the desert," they said in their fear. (Exodus 14:12c, M)

But Moses said, "Have no fear, stand firm and watch how the Eternal will deliver you today." (Exodus 14:13, M)

The answer to their fear was to "march forward."

The various sources become mixed here. The later versions include magic rods, but the earlier one says simply that there was "a strong east wind." It was enough of a hurricane to part the waters of the shallow lake and the Israelites rushed through. By the time the Egyptians could see to follow, the wind had changed. The heavy chariots stuck in the muddy bottom of the lake, and then as the waters came back in a rush into their regular place, the Egyptians were effectively stopped and many were drowned. There may have been torrents of rain and lightning, as Psalm 77 suggests. This is the story that grew into the parting of the Red Sea by waving a divining rod and watching the pillars of fire and the cloud.

The main point in this story is that Yahweh led his people out of Egypt against overwhelming odds, and it was Moses' great faith and courageous leadership that made it possible.

This great story is not the kind that dies or fades away. The memory of the event grew in the minds of the people and was expanded in the retelling. It was an object lesson of Yahweh's concern for His chosen people. "Starting with the fact that it was the oppressor that had been destroyed," Moses "proclaimed that Jahveh hated all oppression and therefore demanded of those whom he had chosen as his people that they be scrupulously just in all their relationships. It was this interpretation that first gave creative meaning to the event."[1]

I.

When the author of the letter to the Hebrews speaks of Christian faith, he recounts the great heroes of the Old Testament. Chief among these is Moses. He finds many events by which Moses "won his record for faith," beginning with the faith of his parents, by which he was saved from death in the bulrushes, and reaching its climax with the crossing of the Red Sea.

This whole list encourages faith on the part of the reader. Moses worked against seemingly insurmountable odds. From the time of Creation, through Abel, Enoch, Noah, Abraham, the patriarchs, and many others, men had withstood all kinds of evil. They were great heroes. Their reputation for faith was excellent. "They all won their record for faith, but the Promise they did not obtain. God had something better in store for us; he would not have them perfected apart from us." (Hebrews 11:39-40, M)

The Promise lies in Christ. The Israelites worshiped God in fear even after the revelation in the desert. Moses was terrified in God's presence. But, says the author of Hebrews, now that the time is at hand and the end of the age is come, we Christians are in the presence of a God of love. He is still the judge, but those who have faith in Christ are saved. For Christ Himself is our sacrifice, and through our faith the Promise may be fulfilled in those who lived

[1] Cuthbert A. Simpson, *Revelation and Response in the Old Testament* (New York: Columbia Univ. Press), pp. 36-37.

too soon. The faith of the heroes of the past has been perfected in us who share Christ's sacrifice.

II.

The story of Moses and the story of the heroes as recorded in Hebrews are brought together in a message for us.

Faith is seen as trust in a righteous God. It is courage in the face of seemingly impossible obstacles. It is creative leadership in the face of the confusion of life. It is putting first things first.

For Moses, it was willingness to risk everything to escape from virtual slavery in Egypt. His people could live after a fashion under the domination of the Pharaohs, but they were not free to worship Yahweh as they would like. They were a subject people in the midst of another race.

Faith also involves the community. Because of faith in Jesus Christ, there is a promise of salvation for all who have gone before. In our faith in Christ, their faith is perfected. Faith is not only individual trust in God, but it also involves the faith community, whereby those in communion with the faithful are also saved.

These two elements, the personal and the communal, are present in the kind of faith we find in our own American forefathers. Among the founders of Jamestown or Plymouth, courage and faith were evident in their willingness to settle a new country. Some of them had a nonreligious faith which expressed itself in the simple desire for adventure, but for others God had led them to the land of promise. It was a venture of faith when our founding fathers outlined a new kind of government, based on faith in God who gives us our inalienable rights. The faith of our pioneers, who endured all kinds of hardship to travel west in the early days, led to the establishment of our frontiers.

America needs that kind of faith today. The "host of witnesses encircling us" includes not only our Jewish forefathers crossing the

Red Sea, not only the saints of the Christian era, who by their faith witnessed to the glory of God, but also our founding fathers establishing a government of the people, by the people, and for the people. So, too, we need to "strip off every handicap, strip off sin with its clinging folds, to run our appointed course with steadiness, our eyes fixed on Jesus as the pioneer and the perfection of faith." (Hebrews 12:1-2a, M)

There can be no such adventurous faith for America unless it is present in individuals in such a way that it becomes the core of the community: first, the community of the faithful in the Church, and then the community of people throughout the nation. The method of the writer of the letter to the Hebrews was to remind his readers of the great men and women of the past who had faith. The call to high adventure that inspired Paul and Barnabas, Augustine and Francis of Assisi, Luther and Calvin, Wesley and Alexander Campbell, Jefferson and Franklin, Lincoln and Lee, comes down to the present day with principles unchanged.

A life of faith like this is the goal of all of us. We are called of God to serve Him in our vocations—faithfully, courageously, and with complete self-giving. It may mean taking such chances as Moses took, risking stubborn resistance on the part of his own people and on the part of the Egyptians in their chariots. It may require vision such as our great statesmen have had, seeing a new kind of society as the answer to men's bondage. It may mean rising to heights of heroism wherever we are, refusing to be bound by the customs of the community. We are surrounded from all the ages of the past by witnesses who have lived in obedience to the will of God, regardless of the cost.

These are those who won "divine approval through their faith" (Hebrews 11:39, VK), and they were "well attested" (RSV), "obtained a good report" (KJ), "won a glowing testimony to their faith" (P), "won their renown" (20), "won their record for faith."

(M) And yet there is a higher example than all of these, for "God has something better in store for us . . . who have our eyes fixed upon Jesus as the pioneer and the perfection of faith." (Hebrews 11:40, 12:2, M)

As we share the way revealed in Jesus Christ, we sing:

> "The countless hosts lead on before,
> I must not fear nor stray;
> With them, the pilgrims of the faith,
> I walk the King's highway." (Hymn 432, stanza 5)

29.

"FOR ZEAL AND ZEST OF LIVING"

THANKSGIVING DAY (FAMILY SERVICE)

PSALM 147; ISAIAH 12:1-6; MATTHEW 6:25-34; HYMNS 137, 313, 148, 276

An eager beaver never stops working. He just keeps digging and building dams across the streams. He has zeal.

An Irishman came to America and obtained a job tearing down an old Protestant church. He wrote back to his Catholic friends in Ireland as follows: "Come to America immediately. I have a job wrecking a Protestant church. Don't tell anyone, but if they only knew it I would tear it down for nothing."[1] He had zeal.

A young man was in love. He wrote: "I could swim the ocean to be with you. I could endure the cold of the North Pole, or cross the burning sands of Africa, or climb the steepest mountain, if only I could be in your arms." He had zeal, but I wonder how much ardor he had, for he added a postscript, "I will be over on Wednesday, if it doesn't rain."[2]

Zeal means enthusiasm. Johnny was enthusiastic about his new football. Jane was enthusiastic about her new doll. The whole family was enthusiastic about their new station wagon. We are all enthusiastic about our Church. We have zeal.

Just to be alive is wonderful. I like it. In fact, I get enthusiastic about it. I have fervor for it. I feel the zeal of living, and on this Thanksgiving Day I think we should all thank God for the zeal of living.

---

[1] Leewin B. Williams, *Encyclopedia of Wit, Humor, and Wisdom* (Nashville: Abingdon-Cokesbury), No. 4116.

[2] *Ibid.*, No. 2319.

Another word we use is zest. When we look at a picture with keen enjoyment, that is zest. When we watch the sun setting, or listen to beautiful music, or see a beautiful horse running, or watch lambs springing around their pastures, this is fun, and we have zest for it all.

I have seen boys and girls dive into a steak with gusto. Or you should see someone go through three hamburgers and top them off with six bottles of pop. That is gusto, or zest. And some of us feel that way about living.

So we say we have a relish for life. Now, sometimes relish refers to a particular brand of pickles, but we also say that we relish something, like strawberry shortcake or a game of baseball. When we relish apple pie, it is because it has a good aftertaste.

Sometimes, we do things that leave a bad taste in our mouths, like soap when the mouth gets washed out, or like a boy who eats too much and gets indigestion, or a man who drinks too much and gets a hangover. There is no zest in that, because the aftereffect is bad.

But when we have a real liking for something—a dog with a friendly face, a bird that sings, a nice home—then we have zest.

And so we say:

> "For zeal and zest of living . . .
> We thank you, Lord, for these." (Hymn 313, stanza 3)

I.

Thanksgiving is a wonderful time of the year, when we count all our blessings. It is when we sing:

> "We thank you, Lord of Heaven,
> For all the joys that greet us,
> For all that you have given
> To help us and delight us
> In earth and sky and seas." (Hymn 313)

Let us count our blessings. What are the joys that have come to your house this past year? Is it a new child in the home? Or is it simply the love that we find among the members of the family? Or is it the friendship of our friends and neighbors? Or did someone do something special that made us grateful? Or is the time we spend at church worth thanking God for?

When we go for a ride in the country and see the sunlight on the meadows, or the rainbow's fleeting wonder, or the clouds with cooling shadows, or the stars that shine in splendor—we thank the Lord for these.

And then on that same drive in the country, we see the swift and gallant horses, the lambs in pastures springing, the dogs with friendly faces, and the birds crowded in the trees and singing and chirping away.

And when we are sick, there are magic medicines. Penicillin can be found in bread, or in green leaves in the river. Castor oil comes from beans. And there are herbs that cool our fevers.

And there are those dinners which we eat with such gusto on Thanksgiving Day. We may get so excited about it that instead of saying that we approach the wonderful goodies with zeal and vigor, we will get our tongues twisted and say, "veal and zigor."

II.

The blessings of life are commonplace. It is the seedtime and the harvest, our life, our health, our food, for which we are thankful.

> "He heals the brokenhearted,
> and binds up their wounds. . . .
> He covers the heavens with clouds,
> he prepares rain for the earth . . .
> He gives to the beasts their food,
> and to the young ravens which
> cry." (Ps. 147:3, 8-9, RSV)

Jesus tells us that the lilies of the field are more glorious than the rich King Solomon in all his robes. The wild birds never put their food away for the winter, and yet God provides for them. But men worry all the time, and become anxious. So Jesus says:

"Don't be anxious about tomorrow. Don't worry about your clothes or your food. Just do what God says, and that is all that God wants us to do. . . . I have come that you might have life, and have it abundantly."

Paul tried to say the same thing in different words: "May the God of hope fill you with all joy and peace in believing, so that by the power of the Holy Spirit you may abound in hope." (Rom. 15:13, RSV)

So we come back to what Jesus was talking about. He really believed in the zeal and zest of living! When we have that, we do not worry about all those other things. And we thank God for the faith and understanding that make it possible for us to have zeal and zest. We have the "words to tell our loving" of God, and so we have "the hope of peace unending."

We know that God loves us, and we know it chiefly because He sent us Jesus Christ. There is not much to thank God for unless we remember that He sent us Jesus Christ to show us how to live. And because we have faith in Jesus Christ, the whole world seems different. At times, the world looks like a sad place with all its stress and strain and wars, but then we remember that it is God's world, and that Jesus came into the world to make it different. Then, even when things go wrong, we can still be thankful because of Jesus Christ.

So we face the wonders of life with keen enthusiasm, and we accept being alive with gusto. As we move through the years we find that the aftertaste is good. This is the kind of zeal and zest for living that comes from real faith and understanding and trust in the God of Jesus Christ.

I want to close with part of a great prayer by Walter Rauschenbusch. As you listen, perhaps you can pray it silently with me:

"O God, we thank thee for this universe, our great home; for its vastness and its riches, and for the manifoldness of the life which teems upon it and of which we are a part. We praise thee for the arching sky and the blessed winds, for the driving clouds and the constellations on high. We praise thee for the salt sea and the running water, for the everlasting hills, and for the grass under our feet. We thank thee for our senses by which we can see the splendor of the morning, and hear the jubilant songs of love, and smell the breath of springtime. Grant us, we pray thee, a heart wide open to all this joy and beauty, and save our souls from being so steeped in care or so darkened by passions, that we pass heedless and unseeing when even the thornbush by the wayside is aflame with the glory of God." [3]

"For zeal and zest of living,
For faith and understanding,
For words to tell our loving,
For hope of peace unending—
We thank you, Lord, for these." (Hymn 313, stanza 3)

---

[3] Walter Rauschenbusch, *Prayers of the Social Awakening* (Boston: Pilgrim Press), p. 47. Used by permission of the publisher.

30.

CHRISTIAN INITIATION

AT A BAPTISM

PSALM 143:1-10; JOSHUA 1:1-9; I TIMOTHY 6:11-19;

HYMNS 408, 186, 466, 579

There is a good deal of mystery surrounding the early rites of initiation into the Christian fellowship. Baptism and Confirmation were not developed into rites which we can recreate until some time in the third century.

We know that Jesus was baptized by John the Baptist, but there is no record of Jesus having baptized anyone. It is likely that the water Baptism of John was the primary source of the Christian rite. "It was a sign and pledge of participation in the Age to Come to those who repented and underwent a moral conversion." [1] It was a preparation for the new kingdom that was coming at the end of the era. It was a rebirth of one's moral character.

The Jewish practice of circumcision contributed to the early meaning of Baptism, and for a time circumcision was a necessary prelude to Baptism. It was the means whereby one was drawn into the community.

The non-Christian world also added to this early picture, for among the Greeks there were mystery cults, where dramatic ceremonies of initiation provided the guarantee of immortality through

[1] Massey H. Shepherd, Jr., *Oxford American Prayer Book Commentary* (New York: Oxford), p. 271.

union with a God who had died and risen again. So when Paul talked about "being baptized into Christ's death, or buried with him in Baptism, that we might be raised with him in glory and in newness of life" (Romans 6:3-4, Colossians 2:11-13), he was using language which adherents of the Greek mystery cults could understand.[2]

Usually Baptism and Confirmation were a single rite in the early days, and catechetical instruction came before Baptism, with both Baptism and Confirmation being administered on the eve of Easter or Pentecost. Normally it was a service for adults only, with the bishop present to administer both rites.

In the fourth century, after Christianity became respectable under Constantine, the Church grew so fast that it became impossible for the bishops to be present. So priests and deacons baptized, and Confirmation took place when the bishop could be present, or sometimes the priest would confirm, using an ointment blessed by the bishop (still the custom in Eastern Orthodox Churches).

Now that Christianity was respectable, it became common practice to baptize infants. The evidence is not clear whether infants were baptized from earliest times. From this time on, however, infant Baptism was common, and there was a gap between the times of Baptism and Confirmation. With this shift, the careful training for Baptism was dropped, and there was practically no catechism until the Reformation when it was restored by Luther, Cranmer, and others.

The earliest form of Baptism is described by Hippolytus of Rome in the third century, before the services were separated. "The service took place towards dawn on Easter or Pentecost, after the lengthy vigil service of psalms, lessons, and prayers. When the water in the font had been blessed, the candidates, stripped of all clothing and

---

[2] *Ibid.*

ornaments, gave to the presbyter the triple renunciations of Satan, his service, and his works, then descended into the font where they made their profession of belief in the words of the Creed. At each profession of faith, in the Father, the Son, and the Holy Spirit, they were baptized by one of the attending clergy. Anointings with blessed oils were made upon each candidate before and after Baptism, but these were carefully distinguished from the chrism by the Bishop which was to follow. After they had put on their clothing, they were immediately brought to the Bishop, who laid his hand upon each one, praying for the gift of the Holy Spirit. He then anointed and sealed each one upon the forehead with the consecrated chrism, and gave each one the kiss of peace. The Holy Communion followed immediately, beginning with the Offertory, and the newly baptized made their first Communion." [3]

With Baptism necessary for salvation, the place of Confirmation, after being separated from Baptism, became confused. Bishops were notoriously lax in administering Confirmation, and no effort was made to provide careful preparation. Children began receiving Communion before being confirmed. Only with the Reformation was any of this straightened out, and even then it was not too clear. Rome still uses chrism and not the laying on of hands at Confirmation, and sometimes this rite is performed by a priest using oil blessed by a bishop. The Episcopal Church, however, said that Confirmation must be by a bishop through the laying on of hands. Cranmer insisted on this, plus adequate preparation by learning the Catechism at the "age of discretion." It was Cranmer who introduced the familiar prayer beginning, "Defend, O Lord, this thy child. . . ."

---

[3] Quoted from *Prayer Book Studies* (New York: Church Pension Fund), pp. 6-7, and Shepherd, *Oxford American Prayer Book Commentary* (New York: Oxford), p. 271. Both of these sources are reflected throughout the sermon. Used by permission of the publishers.

I.

Our present Baptism service still contains many primitive elements, although it has been revised considerably, with the last revision in 1928 combining the infant and adult forms.

The custom of having Baptism as part of the major morning service on a Sunday or holy day is for a very good reason: that the congregation may welcome the newly baptized and may "testify of receiving them." It is also an opportunity for each member of the congregation to remember "his own profession made to God in his Baptism."[4]

The custom of having sponsors goes back to about the third century. The early Church required sponsors for both children and adults, "to testify to the character and sincerity of the candidate, and to assure the Church that he was not a police spy."[5] They also had today's responsibility of watching over the candidate to see that he knew what he ought to know, both before and after Baptism. The American Church is liberal in its acceptance of sponsors, but it is clear that it expects the sponsors to see to the candidate's Christian nurture.

To baptize means literally to dip. When Cranmer prepared the 1549 Prayer Book, the instruction was to immerse the infant three times, unless he was weak and then water was poured on him. In 1552, he needed to be immersed only once. The present English book still prefers dipping, and our American book reads, "shall dip him in the Water discreetly, or shall pour Water upon him."

As a matter of fact, immersion is in almost complete disuse, and Episcopal churches rarely have baptismal tanks. It is usually necessary to borrow a neighboring Baptist or Disciples church if someone wishes immersion. Affusion or pouring can be traced back to

---

[4] Shepherd, *op. cit.,* p. 273.

[5] *Loc. cit.*

the early Church in cases where the water supply was short, the weather bad, or the candidate weak. "The earliest pictorial representations of Baptism show the candidate standing naked in a stream or font while the baptizer pours water over him so that the whole body is washed." [6]

II.

What is the meaning of this great rite of Christian initiation?

It is, first of all, the means to membership in the Church, "the Body of which Jesus Christ is the Head, and all baptized people are the members." Every baptized infant or adult is a member of the holy Church universal, not just a member of the Episcopal Church but of the holy Catholic Church which is mentioned in the Creeds. He is "a member of Christ."

Second, he is made "a Child of God." He has been reborn by the act of the Holy Spirit. Just as he has been born into a human family and as a citizen of this nation, so he is now reborn into the family of God. Just as he is naturally a child of his human parents, so he is adopted as a child of the heavenly Father in a new spiritual relationship.

Third, he is an "inheritor of the kingdom of heaven." He has the promise of eternal life. He is in the company of believers who will receive the gift of Resurrection.

In these ways, the grace of God is mediated to him through the act of the Church. The Church provides sponsors to see that this relationship is maintained, as far as that is humanly possible.

Because infants cannot provide the faith necessary for Baptism, "by the faith of their sponsors, infants are received into Christ's Church, become the recipients of his grace, and are trained in the household of faith."

"More is begun than is effected in Baptism," as Reuel Howe tells

---

[6] *Ibid.*, p. 279.

the College of Preachers.[7] It is the continuing grace of God that makes a child "grow in wisdom and in stature, and in favor with God and man." God acts through the congregation, and especially through the sponsors and the parents, in Baptism. For the infant, the parents are the Church, and they teach through the parent-infant relationships that the God who is at work in their home is the same God whom they meet at church. God is dependable, and the children discover God's love, justice, and dynamic grace because their parents live in relationship to that kind of God in their home.

Baptism is literally an initiation, a starting point, by which God's powers are released to make the child grow spiritually. The next step will be Confirmation, wherein the boy or girl takes on personal responsibility for the promises made in his name by his sponsors. Then comes the great privilege of the first Communion, and the process of initiation is complete.

We are beginning something which will not complete itself for a number of years. Through the parents and sponsors of these infants we are starting a process that they will carry on in their homes, where the Christian faith will be part of the atmosphere, and thus God will work through these children as their sponsors and parents take seriously the incorporation of these infants into the congregation of Christ's flock.

"We receive this child into the congregation of Christ's flock; and do sign him with the sign of the Cross, in token that hereafter he shall not be ashamed to confess the faith of Christ crucified, and manfully to fight under his banner, against sin, the world, and the devil; and to continue Christ's faithful soldier and servant unto his life's end. Amen."

---

[7] See Reuel L. Howe, *Man's Need and God's Action* (Greenwich: The Seabury Press, 1953), pp. 53-61.

31.

"THE MIND OF CHRIST"

THE THEME OF THE SYMPHONY

PSALM 145; JEREMIAH 31:1-14; PHILIPPIANS 2:1-13;

HYMNS 356, 366, 527 (tune 352), 258

Let this mind be in you which was also in Christ Jesus. (KJ)
Treat one another with the same spirit as you experience in Jesus Christ. (M)
Let Christ himself be your example as to what your attitude should be. (P)
Let the same disposition be in you which was in Christ Jesus. (W, 3rd ed.)
Have the same attitude Jesus Christ had. (Phil. 2:5, G)

One of the great phrases describing the source of our inspiration is found in the text, "Have this mind among yourselves, which you have in Christ Jesus." (RSV) Phillips Brooks summed it up this way, "To seek for the reproduction of Christ's mind in the mind of the community is the greatest aim that we can cherish."[1] It is often suggested that the mind of Christ is the clue to our behavior, to the work of the nation, to understanding the Bible.

This is all very true, but when we discover that for many people the phrase has no meaning, we need to clarify our thoughts. I pro-

[1] Quoted by Wade Crawford Barclay, *Challenge and Power* (Nashville: Abingdon-Cokesbury), p. 105.

pose that we look at five different translations of the text upon which this phrase is based, with the hope that we may see more clearly what is implied.

I.

Paul's use of "the mind of Christ" is a reminder of the significance of truth in our ethical judgments. It means that we should know what Jesus taught (as found in the first three Gospels), how the Gospels impressed the early Church, and how the Holy Spirit guides us today. For example, "in estimating the relative spiritual value of different portions of the Bible, the standard is the Mind of Christ as unfolded in the experience of the Church and appropriated by the individual Christian through His Spirit."[2] Archbishop Temple calls this having the "mind of God." He says, "The truth of things is what they are in the mind of God, and it is only when we act according to the mind of God that we are acting in accordance with the truth, in accordance with reality. Everything else is making a mistake."[3]

This truth is good news, for the mind of Christ is a Gospel. It is the truth that God sent Jesus Christ to save us, direct us, and give us power. When we by faith have the mind of Christ, we are able to correct our own judgments in the light of eternal truth. We know we can have the mind of Christ by reading the Gospel in faith, but this does not tell us what it is in any given circumstance.

II.

"Treat one another with the same spirit as you experience in Christ Jesus," says Moffatt's translation. This turns our thinking in another direction. We not only read about Christ and listen to

---

[2] *Doctrine in the Church of England* (New York: Macmillan), p. 32.
[3] *Daily Readings from William Temple* (London: Hodder and Stoughton), No. 1075.

His words, we come into an experience of Him. We find in Him a spirit of humility, service, and obedience.

In the same passage in which we find our text, there follows a description of how Christ emptied himself of all deity and became a man. Then in perfect humility, He acted as a servant and was perfectly obedient to His heavenly Father, even though it meant death.

It is this spirit that is the goal of Christian behavior. We see this spirit at its best in such Christian saints as Brother Lawrence, as he washed dishes in a monastery and wrote his *Practice of the Presence of God*. We see the "same spirit as you experience in Christ Jesus" in the utter devotion of a Francis of Assisi as he worked with single heart and mind to serve his Master. We see this spirit to some extent whenever people are big-hearted or sacrificial or self-abasing or courageous. There are people living close to the spirit of the Beatitudes who are the saints of God in this twentieth century, and you can meet them anywhere.

"If any man would come after me, let him deny himself and take up his cross and follow me. For whoever would save his life will lose it, and whoever loses his life for my sake will find it. For what will it profit a man, if he gains the whole world and forfeits his life? Or what shall a man give in return for his life?" (Matt. 16:24-26, RSV)

III.

"Let Christ himself be your example as to what your attitude should be," says the translation by Phillips. Christ, then, is an example. Thomas á Kempis wrote a famous devotional manual called *The Imitation of Christ*. The best seller outside the Bible in America was *In His Steps*. "Our hope is that we should be as Jesus."

Now this does not mean that we should be literal imitators. We do not need to be carpenters, wandering prophets, or bachelors.

We do not need to believe that Moses wrote the books of the Law, or that demons are real, or that the end of the world is coming in this generation, although Jesus clearly believed these things.

The example of Christ is in terms of general principles. We find them in such statements as: "love your neighbor as yourself," "do unto others as you would have them do unto you," "forgive unto seventy times seven," "thy faith hath made thee whole." We find His example in His forgiving the harlot, healing the demoniac, courageously facing the high priests and Pilate.

Some of us who are excellent carpenters may not have the spirit of Christ, and certainly some who cannot saw through a piece of wood may be members of the kingdom of God. You may recall how Paul wrote that there are varieties of aptitudes, and our task is to "walk worthy of the vocation wherewith we are called." The vocation of Jesus was different from our vocation, but the demand for obedience to God's will is basic to all. "The fundamental difference between Jesus and other men lies in his power to create a new humanity in his own image, after his likeness. If we ever get to be like him, it will be through him."[4] These words of Professor Drown show how Jesus can be an example and our Saviour at the same time.

IV.

"Let the same disposition be in you which was in Christ Jesus," says Weymouth's translation (third edition). Christian behavior is a matter of disposition. Sour-faced Christians are not particularly winsome or lovable. The man who has faith in Christ is of a winning and cheerful disposition. He does not let anything get him down, no matter how serious it may be.

The example of Jesus in the Gospel stories stands out. He is al-

---

[4] E. S. Drown, *The Creative Christ* (New York: Macmillan), p. 125.

ways pictured as a mature and poised person, ready for whatever life may offer Him. He is cheerful when life calls for cheerfulness, and He is capable of accepting suffering even though His soul or body may be in agony. He is not lacking in emotional response, but always they are under some degree of control. He may agonize until the sweat rolls down as blood, and He may pray to God when it seems as if God has forsaken Him. And yet there is a victorious spirit underlying all that He does.

Dependability of emotional response is significant for Christian living. It is hard to live with people who cannot be counted on. They do not react consistently to personal relations or impersonal stimuli. They may accept us cheerfully one time and curse us the next. They allow their physical condition, their emotional fatigue, or their psychological frustrations to dictate to their wills.

But if we have the same disposition in us which was in Christ Jesus, we shall find that we will be consistent in our love towards others. Our dispositions will reflect the objective situation rather than our own internal turmoil, for there is no internal turmoil when faith has cast out fear.

V.

A fifth and final way of putting the mind of Christ is Goodspeed's translation: "Have the same attitude that Christ Jesus had." An attitude is a way of thinking, acting, or feeling. Here again we turn to the example of Jesus in the Gospels. Can we think, or feel, or act in the manner He did?

When He thought, His first question was, "What is God's will for me?" This was always the highest and best that He knew. It depended on His education, His knowledge of the Old Testament, His own personal insights, and on the personal relations which were at stake. The Law could be overturned if human need demanded it. There was no thought of personal safety, but of His mission as the Son of God.

When He responded emotionally, He always asked, "What is the response of love to this person?" Self-giving love, the service which is perfect freedom, willingness to lose His life, and sensing of human need were the basic motives. The ready sympathy of the Good Samaritan, the immediate reaction of the shepherd whose sheep has wandered, the rejoicing over the finding of a lost coin, the providing of life lived abundantly, and the readiness to forgive were at the depth of His emotional being.

When He acted, He did so in terms of His own admonition: "Seek ye first the kingdom of God, and his righteousness; and all these things shall be added unto you." (Matt. 6:33, KJ) He resisted temptation, and He had greater temptations than we do because His power was greater. He was instantly obedient, even though the result might mean His death.

An attitude is always a source of power. Because the attitude of Jesus Christ is primarily an attitude of complete trust in God, God responds with His grace, which is the power to do His will.

VI.

The mind or spirit or example or disposition or attitude which was in Christ Jesus, can be in us!

It is not an ideal which we hold in front of us. There is no law by which this goal can be attained. It comes to us through devotion to the God who sent Jesus Christ. It comes to us because God worked through Christ to reconcile the world to Himself. It is no virtue of ours that the mind of Christ comes alive in us, "for it is by grace you have been saved, as you had faith; it is not your doing but God's gift, not the outcome of what you have done, . . . therefore, . . . live a life worthy of your calling." (Eph. 2:8-9; 4:1, M)

We can sing:

"Let this mind be in us which was in thee,
Who wast a servant that we might be free,
Humbling thyself to death on Calvary." (Hymn 366, stanza 3)

Because Jesus is not simply someone who lived and died many centuries ago, the mind of Christ is not a fact of history alone. We believe in the risen and living Christ, and through our devotion to Him He will impart his mind to us.

"O living Christ, who still
Dost all our burdens share,
Come now and dwell within the hearts
Of all men everywhere!" (Hymn 527, stanza 4)

So we say that "Christ is the world's true Light" (Hymn 258), for He is the beacon who stands in the darkness to lead us home. We become "heirs of God and joint heirs with Christ" because we give ourselves to God through Him.

So now we know what we mean by the mind of Christ. It is the central theme of Christian living, the melody of our reaction to *A Symphony of the Christian Year*. It is the focal point of our thinking and feeling and acting. But above all, Christ Himself is the source of power by which we can achieve the purpose of this great phrase:

"Let this attitude be yours, which was also in Christ Jesus." (VK)

INDEX

(The more important items are in *italics*)

BIBLICAL REFERENCES

85-154-12-C